PRINCE OF FENCES

IKEY SOLOMONS,

From a Sketch taken at the Lambeth Street Police Office.

Prince of Fences

The Life and Crimes
of
Ikey Solomons

J. J. TOBIAS

With a foreword by
EWEN MONTAGU

VALLENTINE, MITCHELL—LONDON

First published in Great Britain in 1974 by

VALLENTINE, MITCHELL & CO. LTD.

67 Great Russell Street

London WC1B 3BT

Copyright © 1974 by J. J. Tobias

ISBN 0 85303 174 6

Printed in Great Britain by
Unwin Brothers Limited
The Gresham Press
Old Woking Surrey

CONTENTS

LIST OF PLATES

Following page 66

FOREWORD

The interest that one finds in real crime, crime in real life, is not mainly concerned either with the offence or with the detection, or even, except in rare instances, with the trial. In real life the detection is almost always either simple or lucky or the result of tedious and painstaking, albeit skilled, enquiries—or occasionally a combination of one or more of those. In real life there is seldom much thrill even in the trial; apart from the mass of necessary but unexciting evidence on peripheral matters the result can be foreseen at an early stage.

The fascination of crime in real life is far more concerned with the offender. Not 'Whodunit' or even how did he do it, but why did he do it? Even to those of us who have tried cases the real interest came at the end of each trial, after the verdict, and that interest remained absorbing even after trying some thousands of cases. For, in all of those thousands of cases it is safe to say that the cause of the offence was never the same; in some the motive was the same in each case but the temporary or basic background of the offender which caused him or her to succumb would differ—or it might be the other way round. And factors of that kind are of vital importance in deciding what should be the sentence or order. Has he become a professional criminal or not? If he has, why has he? And how can one dissuade him from continuing or otherwise protect the public?

In those circumstances all who are interested in crime and penology find a fascination in past history. A professional criminal today has become one for a variety of reasons—how do those reasons compare with those of his predecessors? What was his upbringing, his training and his progress in his profession—and can any useful deductions be drawn from the past?

The interest of old time penology is quite different. Apart from capital punishment virtually the only sentences possible in the late 18th and early 19th centuries were imprisonment or transportation, but the details of what these really meant are of absorbing interest. Most of us know something of the sordid and brutalising conditions of prisons before the first prison-reformers but how many of us know such details as that, even after acquittal, someone held in prison could not obtain his release at all until he had paid the appropriate fees (not inconsiderable fees at contemporary wage-levels) to various minor officials?

And what did a sentence of transportation mean and involve? When I was Chairman of Middlesex Sessions we used to get a steady flow of requests for information from Australians—'My great-great-grandfather was transported to Australia after conviction at Middlesex Sessions in 18—; could you please let me know what he was convicted of'. Generally we could find the answer, though we usually felt that great-great-grandpapa's offence was so trivial that it would come as a disappointment to our enquirer. But even then I little realised that very many of those transported might well have been ancestors of whom their descendants could not unreasonably have been genuinely proud— for many of them were not thugs, recidivists or hardened criminals (as is the general impression) but were men with good qualities to whom courts nowadays might well have given a chance on probation—and who made good in Australia in spite of the suffering that they endured before and after their voyage— nor did I realise how one might see the predecessor of our system of parole operated more than a century earlier by enlightened authorities in Australia and Tasmania.

But what has all this got to do with a book entitled *Prince of Fences: The Life and Crimes of Ikey Solomons*'? Dr. Tobias has had the excellent idea of recounting the engrossing story of the man who had not only earned that 'proud' title but also, perhaps an even greater accolade, such fame that successors could almost compete for the title of 'another Ikey Solomons'—and not only of recounting that story but of explaining in fascinating detail the background that made him what he was, and the system that imprisoned him three times. And Ikey Solomons' own story is well worth-while in itself; few men from his beginnings could have amassed the fortune that he did, fewer would have managed to escape from custody while awaiting transportation, and still fewer would have done what he then did—

joined his wife in Tasmania, to which place she had meanwhile herself been transported, and so risked the almost inevitable eventual arrest and carrying into effect of his own sentence— what a man!

Few people have the knowledge of the criminal-criminological-penological side of that period that Dr. Tobias has and fewer could bring it to life as the background of the story of a really fascinating rogue.

Ewen Montagu

AUTHOR'S PREFACE

In the first fifty or sixty years of the nineteenth century the level of crime in England, and especially London, was probably higher than at any other time (including the present day). In 1815 Britain had just led the rest of Europe to success in the fight against Napoleon and was in the early stages of the industrial growth that made her the dominant power of the century. Yet whole streets of the capital were notorious as the abode of criminals whose activities were for long unchecked by the rudimentary police of the day, and juvenile delinquency, though much studied and much bemoaned, was little affected by the efforts of the law-enforcement agencies. Though there were reforms of police and prisons and in other spheres which affected crime and criminals, it was not until the 1850s and 1860s that dramatic drops in the level of criminality occurred.

Despite the predominance of this period in our criminal history, none of the ordinary criminals of the day, it seems to me, are known by name to the general public. Burke and Hare are still remembered by some people, but they were Resurrection men who stole human bodies for dissection, specialists meeting a particular need—and, be it noted, medical education would have been the poorer without their efforts. They are as different from those I have in mind as other murderers who from time to time catch the public imagination with crimes that are indeed interesting but are exceptional and thus tell us nothing about everyday, humdrum crime.

The criminals who are part of common knowledge come from earlier periods—Dick Turpin and his fellow-highwaymen, Jack Sheppard and Jonathan Wild, are seventeenth century figures—or from later ones—Charley Peace, the burglar turned murderer, was hanged in 1879.

Isaac Solomons may perhaps fill the gap. He was engaged in ordinary crime, even if he was an exceptional man who had some extraordinary adventures, and I hope that his story will give some picture of crime and criminal life in his day, and of society's reaction to it. In any event, it does, I hope, make a good tale.

Many people have helped in the preparation of this book. Much of the evidence comes from official records here and in Tasmania. I am grateful to the staff of the Public Record Office in London for willing assistance over several years. Crown copyright, I should add, is reserved in extracts from official records quoted here. I owe a deep debt to the former Principal Archivist of Tasmania, Mr. P. R. Eldershaw, and to his successor Mr. M. J. Saclier; Mr. J. F. H. Moore, M.A., of Hobart, like those two gentlemen, helped considerably in the difficult task of archival research at long distance. Other Australian scholars who have helped include Mr. R. S. Sharman, Dr. L. L. Robson, Dr. G. Bergman and Dr. A. P. Joseph. The Rev. J. Sunshine, Honorary Archivist to the United Synagogue, kindly traced relevant entries in the records in his care; Mr. R. J. D'Arcy Hart of the Jewish Museum advised me too. The editors of the *Australian Dictionary of Biography* supplied me with information. Part of the final chapter first appeared in the pages of the *Dickensian*. I am grateful to the staffs of the Greater London Record Office, and of the Office of the High Comissioner for Australia in London.

Finally, I should mention those who first enabled me to put together my thoughts on Ikey Solomons. I first spoke about him to the Henry Fielding Society at the Police College, and have had the benefit of many talks about him and his world with the first Chairman of that Society, Mr. P. J. Stead, O.B.E., M.A., F.R.S.L., Dean of Academic Studies at the College. Ikey was first introduced to the wider public in a broadcast on BBC Radio 4, and my decision to turn him into a book came in a discussion with the two men who helped with that broadcast, Mr. Patrick Harvey the producer and Mr. David Brierley who provided the 'voices' needed. To them and to all the others mentioned I am truly grateful.

J. J. Tobias

The Police College,
Bramshill House,
Nr. Basingstoke, Hants.

Chapter One

IKEY SOLOMONS

Isaac Solomons, the hero or villain of this book, reached the peak of his fame in July, 1830, when he stood in the dock at the Old Bailey facing thirteen charges of theft and receiving stolen goods. He had had a similar experience twenty years before: in June, 1810, he had been sentenced to transportation for life for picking pockets. He was not, in fact, sent out of the country as a result of this sentence, and in 1816 he was released from imprisonment. In the next ten years he built up for himself a position as one of London's leading fences ('the great Ikey Solomons', he was called), the bubble being pricked by a search of his home in 1826 and his arrest in 1827. This resourceful man then escaped from custody and managed to get out of England, eventually joining his wife in Van Diemen's Land (the modern Tasmania), where she had gone as a convict—for between Ikey's two trials at the Old Bailey, his wife and his father had stood in the same place. Both were sentenced on the same day in 1827, although their offences were not connected. Ikey was recognized as an escaped prisoner on his arrival in Van Diemen's Land and, after a great legal battle which attracted much attention, he was shipped back to England to stand trial. Convicted on two of the thirteen charges in July, 1830, he returned to Van Diemen's Land the following year as a convict. He and his wife were eventually reunited—but only to quarrel and separate. Ikey died a poor and lonely man in 1850. That, in outline, is the story of this book.

Isaac Solomons was a man of medium height—five feet nine inches, according to the register of Newgate Prison. His build is there described as 'slender' and his complexion as 'dark'; he had brown hair and hazel eyes. When he escaped and was a hunted man, a handbill described him as of 'sallow complexion' and 'acquiline nose', while someone who knew him well said he was 'a tall man, thin, with a long visage, dark hair and eyes, sharp hooked nose'. Other witnesses described Ikey as 'stooping'. If the drawing of him published in one of the accounts of his life and reproduced facing title page is accurate, he was not of distinctively Jewish appearance. Certainly he was able to pass under such non-Jewish names as Jones or Slowman without attracting remark.

Ikey was probably born about the year 1785 and thus was about forty-five years old when he appeared at the Old Bailey in 1830. It is true that at other times he gave for himself ages which would suggest different dates of birth. In 1810 he said that he was twenty-one and in 1828 that he was fifty, although it seems probable that he was in fact about twenty-five in 1810 (he was then a married man with a son about two years old) and forty-three in 1828. But we can guess at reasons why he might have departed from the truth on these two occasions. In 1810 he was awaiting trial for a serious offence and might well have thought that the younger he could represent himself to be, the easier would be his fate. In 1828 he was pleading for his wife to be released from imprisonment and might well have thought that to add a few years to his age would increase his chances of success.

Ikey was the son of Henry Solomons, who was born in Wurzburg, Bavaria, in about 1758. Henry came to England as a young man, and one of the accounts of Ikey's life says that his father made his living by acting as a merchant buying on commission for 'the great Goldsmidt'—presumably Abraham or Benjamin Goldsmid. These two brothers were bankers who played a major part in financing Britain's government loans during the Napoleonic Wars. Benjamin committed suicide in 1808 as a result of business troubles. In 1809 Abraham financed a £14 million loan by his own credit, but the strain was too much and he too took his own life, in 1810. Henry Solomons may have been employed by one or other Goldsmid, but when he appeared for trial at the Old Bailey on a charge of stealing jewellery, he gave his occupation as 'dealer', a vague description which could cover a multitude of things. His daughter said he was a glass-engraver, and that may have been his main means of earning his livelihood. On coming to England from Bavaria, Henry settled in the East End of London, in the cluster of streets which, then as now, had a high proportion of Jewish inhabitants. In 1827 he lived at 24 Gravel Lane, Houndsditch, and it may have been there that Ikey was born: he seems to have been born in Gravel Lane or in Cutler Street, which was then a turning off Gravel Lane. Ikey's place of birth cannot be pinpointed with sufficient accuracy for the Greater London Council to place one of their commemorative blue plaques outside it, in the unlikely event of their wishing to do so, but we can be sure that he was born and grew up in the tangle of streets between Aldgate Pump and Petticoat Lane. A sister, Sarah, and a brother, Benjamin, were alive in 1827, and so too was Ikey's mother, then seventy-three years old and thus some four years older than her husband.

Ikey's wife and partner in crime was Hannah, known as Ann, the daughter of Moses Julian, who was a coachmaster living in Aldgate. Ann was born in Whitechapel and was probably a year or two younger than Ikey. She too gave a false age when she followed her husband into Newgate Prison—in 1827 she said that she was thirty-four years old, but as her eldest child was about twenty years old at the time, she had presumably taken advantage of the lady's privilege of under-estimating her age. Ann Solomons was five feet, one inch tall, and when she entered Newgate her build was ungallantly described as 'stoutish'. It is true, of course, that she was then some forty years old and the mother of six children. Her complexion was described as 'dark', and she had black hair and hazel eyes. We know nothing more of her appearance but that she dressed well. When she appeared in court in 1827, the *Morning Chronicle* said she was most elegantly dressed, and *The Times* agreed: 'Her dress was quite fashionable, with nothing of the tawdry about it, and exhibited a good deal of solid value.' She certainly had captivated Ikey, for he went through considerable hardship and ran great risks to join her in Van Diemen's Land, and he wrote about her in extravagant terms as 'an innocent, artless and unaffecting wife'. Ikey was ultimately abandoned by the woman of whom he thought so highly and, at the age of forty-five or so, she became the mistress of another man—but that and many other adventures lay far in the future when the couple were married in the Great Synagogue, Duke's Place, London, on 7th January, 1807.

Isaac and Ann had six children. Their eldest son, John, was born in 1807 and Moses followed in 1810, the year of Isaac's first conviction at the Old Bailey and his first imprisonment (or the first that we know about). David was born in 1819 and two daughters followed—Nancy, known subsequently as Anne, on 12th January, 1820, and Sarah on 4th October, 1823. The youngest of the family was Mark, born in 1826, the year his father had to escape hurriedly from his home to avoid arrest. (The dates of birth of most of the children could be a year earlier or later than those given, as only in the case of the two girls has it been possible to find a record of their birth.) Ann Solomons had thus twice had the experience of being left with an infant to care for while her husband could not be with her because of conflict with the law.

The first major interruption to the Solomonses' married life came in 1810. On 17th April Isaac was arrested in Westminster Hall, in company with one Joel Joseph. They were charged with 'feloniously stealing . . . from the person of Thomas Dodd' a pocket-book, value 4s., and its contents (notes to the value of £40 and a cheque for £56), that is, with picking a pocket. A meeting of the electors of Westminster was being held that day to discuss the arrest by order of the House of Commons of one of the members of Parliament representing the City, Sir Francis Burdett. Burdett was a wealthy Radical who, as part of his attack on the privileges of Parliament, had had one of his speeches published—and the publication of words uttered in the House of Commons at that time constituted a breach of privilege. The meeting provoked by Burdett's arrest, held in New Palace Yard in front of Westminster Hall, was described by *The Times* as perhaps the most numerous meeting ever held in London. Such an occasion presented a valuable opportunity to pickpockets, and the newspaper commented that 'the light-fingered fraternity, as might be expected, were very numerous and active'. However, Solomons and Joseph had overlooked the fact that detectives as well as pickpockets attended meetings of this sort, and they were recognized as they left the scene of operations. As *The Times* put it: 'Having made a plentiful harvest, they endeavoured to make their retreat through Westminster Hall; but, unfortunately for them, the doors at the upper end, one leading to the passage of the House of Commons, and the other into Old Palace Yard, were locked, and there was no possibility of escape, a detachment of the Bow-Street Corps being close at their heels.' The pair were seized as they stood dividing the spoils.

John Vickery, a detective of the Worship Street Police Office, had seen the two pickpockets leaving the meeting and going into Westminster Hall. Guessing that this meant that they had made a successful raid, he called John Preston, a member of the Bow Street Patrol, to go with him as he followed the two men. When the officers got to the door of Westminster Hall, they saw Joseph standing with a number of bank notes in his hand as if in the act of counting them. Solomons was near him. Vickery went towards them, and when Joseph saw him he began to run away. Preston ran after Joseph and seized him. Vickery took hold of Solomons and, as he did so, something dropped to his feet—it turned out to be a pocket-book. Vickery thought that Joseph had put something into his mouth and called out to Preston that he should not let him swallow anything, but Preston found that Joseph had nothing in his mouth. Joseph refused to be searched by Preston, saying 'Vickery shall search me, he has known me a good while, and whatever he finds he will return me.' The implication of the remark, rightly or wrongly, is that not all law enforcement officers could be trusted to give back to a prisoner any valuables found on him which did not afterwards form the subject of a charge. When Vickery searched Joseph, he found that he had not been putting the proceeds of the crime into his mouth but had attempted to hide them by stuffing them inside the handkerchief round his neck. There Vickery found three bank notes, for £30, £5, and £2. The pocket-book which Solomons had dropped was found to contain, amongst other things, a cheque for £56, and it was this which made it possible to find the victim of the crime. The cheque was endorsed 'Mr Dodd, Eltham', and a message was accordingly sent to Eltham by a coach going that way. The owner of the pocket-book, Thomas Dodd, an ironmonger's agent, then came to the Bow Street Office to identify his property, and the evidence against Solomons and Joseph was complete.

The next step was for the accused to be brought before a magistrate. In 1810, just as today, those accused of a serious crime had the right to trial by jury and, again just as today, they had also the right to a speedy examination of their case by a magistrate, who was required to satisfy himself that a *prima facie* case existed against the prisoner and that his continued detention was justified. The magistrate would hear the evidence for the prosecution and, if he found it sufficient to require a trial before a jury, he would commit the prisoner to the next sitting of the appropriate court. Of course, the magistrate was not required to reach a decision straight away and he could remand a prisoner for further enquiries before deciding whether to commit him for trial or discharge him. Ikey and his companion suffered no delay, however, and the case was disposed of in one sitting. Solomons and Joseph appeared before John Nares, a magistrate of the Bow Street Office, on 19th April, 1810, two days after their arrest in Westminster Hall. The magistrate heard the story of the arrest from Vickery and confirming evidence from a passerby, who had witnessed the arrest and seen Solomons drop the pocket-book which Vickery had picked up. The victim came to the court to give evidence that the property found on Solomons and Joseph was his and that he had lost his pocket-book whilst at the meeting in New Palace Yard, Westminster. The magistrate accordingly found that a *prima facie* case existed against the two prisoners, and they were committed to stand their trial at the Old Bailey. They were duly lodged in Newgate Prison the same day.

Solomons and Joseph had appeared before a salaried magistrate, a full-time professional employee of the State. Most magistrates in England today are unpaid officers acting from a sense of public duty, and the situation was basically the same in 1810. Then as now, most prisoners appeared before two or more unpaid justices of the peace. However, salaried magistrates had been introduced in the London area in the eighteenth century, because of the impossibility of finding enough unpaid justices of the right quality.

The idea of paid magistrates can be traced back to Tudor days. At least from the time of Elizabeth I there was in London a magistrate, usually known as the Court Justice, who was paid a salary from secret service funds. He was employed by the government on a variety of tasks which demanded the powers of a justice of the peace—tasks which could have been done by a Secretary of State but were perhaps beneath the dignity of so great a man, or perhaps could not safely be done by a leading politician who was much in the public eye. The Court Justice was engaged only for part of his time on these duties, and as far as the public knew he was just one of the magistrates of London. The developments which concern us began when Henry Fielding was appointed Court Justice in 1748, and it was his transformation of the office into one concerned with the active pursuit of crime that has led posterity to regard him as the leading pioneer of police reform in London. There were, of course, honest and disinterested magistrates before Henry Fielding, but it has to be accepted that most of those who dealt with the minor criminal matters of the metropolis were not worthy of that description. The increasing burden of work, both criminal and civil,which fell to the lot of the unpaid justice of the peace had meant that by the eighteenth century it was extremely difficult to find in the London area a sufficient number of men to perform the duty. In the City of London itself, the one square mile within the boundaries which had not changed since the Norman Conquest, there was no problem of this sort. The Lord Mayor himself sat daily at the Mansion House hearing criminal cases. (Ikey's father appeared there in 1827.) The alder-

men of the City in rotation manned another daily court at the
Guildhall. But outside the City there were no civic dignitaries
of this kind who could be prevailed upon to do this arduous
work in exchange for their titles and honours. In consequence,
a class of magistrate had grown up, men entitled perhaps only
by courtesy to the rank of gentleman, who were known as
trading justices—because they made a living by the fees which
they charged for granting summonses or warrants, for releasing
a prisoner and for a whole host of other things. The Court
Justice was a trading justice like the others for most of his time.
Henry Fielding's innovation was that he did not seek to promote
the greatest possible flow of business through his office in order
to augment his income from fees, but devoted his attention to the
reduction of the amount of crime in his area.

From the days of Henry Fielding, there was at Bow Street
first one and then subsequently more than one salaried magistrate,
and from Fielding's day the payment to the magistrate was not
made from secret funds but was an openly avowed payment to a
public official. Before Ikey Solomons was born the Bow Street
Office had become the main police court of London, with a
number of magistrates on its bench. The advantages of stipendiary
magistrates over trading justices were so great that, in 1792, the
trading justice was eliminated from London; seven additional
police offices modelled on that at Bow Street were established
in other parts of the metropolis, with three stipendiary magistrates sitting daily at each of them. The trading justices, like the
other unpaid justices of the peace in the areas of Middlesex
concerned, continued to have the right to act as magistrates, but
their old practices were stopped by a regulation which only
allowed fees to be charged by the magistrates at the police
offices, who paid them into the official funds. This effectively
ended the trading justice, leaving the unpaid justices to carry on
doing their duty as a public service if they wished. In this way
arose the system of the present day, in which there are courts
manned by stipendiary magistrates alongside those manned by
unpaid justices of the peace. In the early nineteenth century, as
today, a stipendiary magistrate was given greater powers than

his unpaid colleagues, and one stipendiary magistrate sitting alone could perform tasks which could only be done by two or more unpaid justices acting together. This included the role of examining magistrate, and this is why Ikey Solomons and Joel Joseph had appeared before a stipendiary magistrate sitting alone.

In 1810, the police offices were at Queen Square and Great Marlborough Street in Westminster; at Hatton Garden, Holborn; at Worship Street, Finsbury Square; at Lambeth Street, White-chapel; and at High Street, Shadwell; all these were in Middlesex, and there was another at Union Street, Southwark, in Surrey. (Various members of the Solomons family were later to appear at Lambeth Street.) An eighth office, the Thames Police Office, at Wapping, created in 1800, was concerned with the policing of the River. The offices were open from ten in the morning until eight at night, and two of the three magistrates of each office were supposed to be there at any one time. However, Henry Goddard, a police officer of the day whose memoirs have recently been published, described the magistrates as sitting 'from eleven o'clock in the morning till three o'clock in the afternoon and again from seven to eight o'clock in the evening'. Indeed, the magistrates of the Hatton Garden Office in 1813, when making regulations about the way in which their officers should report their proceedings, leave us grounds to suppose that they did not always arrive even by 11. Each officer was required to keep a daily diary 'and produce it by eleven o'clock the succeeding morning to the Messenger, who shall lay it before the Magistrate of the day, upon his first coming into the Office'—one gathers that provided the messenger had the book by 11, he could be sure of giving it to the magistrate on his arrival at the office.

At the time of Ikey Solomons's arrest in 1810, not all the police magistrates were barristers, but from 1812 no-one was appointed to the post unless he had that qualification. The salary of the post was at that time £500 a year, which was not regarded as sufficient to attract men of the appropriate quality. In 1821 the salary was raised to £600 a year, but even that did not seem enough. In 1825, Robert Peel, Secretary of State for the Home Department, asked the House of Commons 'whether six hundred a year, the present salary, is sufficient to induce a barrister to give up the emoluments of private practice and the hope of preferment in his profession, to undertake the duties of a magistrate, which requires their almost constant attendance'. Some people were not very happy about the quality of the men who did become stipendiary magistrates, but none the less the measures of 1792 had greatly improved the administration of minor justice in London.

Now that the magistrate at Bow Street had found that a *prima facie* case existed against Solomons and Joseph and had committed them to stand their trial at the Old Bailey, the elaborate process of a prosecution for felony had begun. The next stage in the proceedings was for a bill of indictment to be drawn up. This could be an expensive procedure, as fees had to be paid to the Clerk of the Peace of the county for his trouble. The fees were to be paid by the prosecutor—that is to say, the victim of the crime. In England today most prosecutions are in theory brought by a private individual, who lays an accusation before the Queen's Justices; in fact, in almost every case, the prosecutor is a police officer or other public official acting in his capacity as such. In the early nineteenth century the position was quite different. It was not a mere matter of form that prosecutions were launched by private persons. It was left to the victim of the crime to act as prosecutor and he would have to devote a considerable amount of time to this task. He would have to attend the hearing before the magistrates, which might well be adjourned once or more. He would have to attend before the Clerk of the Peace to obtain a bill of indictment. He would then have to attend the sessions when the prisoner came up for trial, being there on the first day and often having to wait for several days until the case came on, not daring to go far away lest it was called in his absence. Not only was a considerable amount of time required; money had to be laid out for the fees which had to be paid at various stages. However, the prosecutor could hope to obtain a refund of his expenses if he was successful. Despite this, on the whole the prosecution of offenders was a troublesome and an expensive business and we can hardly be surprised that, as was frequently grumbled at the time, many people decided not to throw good money after bad and did not bother to prosecute. There were indeed a number of associations for the prosecution of felons—people would pay a guinea or two a year to be a member of such an association, which would take upon itself the trouble and the expense of prosecuting anyone who stole from a member.

Prisoners against whom a bill of indictment had been prepared had next to appear before the Grand Jury at the beginning of the sessions or assizes. The Grand Jury was a jury of presentment, the original form of jury as it had been brought to England by the Normans. Originally, the jury had been an administrative device. A number of local inhabitants with knowledge of the facts were called before royal commissioners to answer questions on the subject-matter of the inquiry—Domesday Book is made up of the reports of juries. In much the same way, juries were called together to inform the King's Justices whether anyone in their area was accused of robbery or murder or theft. This jury of presentment eventually became known as the Grand Jury, to distinguish it from the petty jury which, as it still does today, determined whether the accused was guilty or not. By Ikey's day the Grand Jury no longer consisted of people who knew the facts of the case themselves. Witnesses gave evidence before the Grand Jury, which consisted of householders, usually of the tradesmen class in London and Middlesex, twenty-five in all. On the first days of the sessions or assizes, the prosecutor for each bill of indictment and his witnesses had to appear before the Grand Jury, giving their evidence so that it could decide whether a *prima facie* case existed against the accused. If the Grand Jury felt that the prisoner should stand his trial, it found a 'true bill'. If it decided that there was no case to answer, it rejected the bill, and the prisoner went free. In the language of the courts, the Jury was then said to have 'ignored' the bill—from the Latin phrase 'ignoramus', meaning 'we do not know anything against the prisoner', which used to be written on the bill. Many of those concerned with the criminal law were critical of the Grand Jury system even in Ikey's day, for it represented an additional stage which served no useful purpose but increased the cost and difficulty of prosecution. Moreover, it provided an excellent opportunity for professional criminals to secure their discharge, because it was much easier to introduce false evidence into the Grand Jury room, where witnesses were heard in secret, than in open court. Moreover, the case was not 'opened' to the Grand Jury—there were no counsel present to explain the matter to them, and they had to piece the story together as best they could from the evidence of the prosecution witnesses. Despite these criticisms, the system long outlived Ikey, not being abolished until 1933. (The Grand Jury still exists in the United States of America.)

Prisoners against whom the Grand Jury had found a true bill then appeared for trial before a petty jury, a trial which in principle was conducted much as it is today. There were, however, a number of differences. First, prisoners accused of felony had only limited rights to employ counsel. Those accused of treason or of the lesser crimes which came into the category of a misdemeanour had the right to counsel, much as now. However, if the prisoner was accused of felony, counsel could merely advise him and assist him in the examination of witnesses; the prisoner himself had to make any address to the court on his own behalf. Only in 1836 was this limitation removed. It was not until much later in the century that the prisoner was allowed to give evidence in his own defence if he wished: until 1898 the prisoner could in no circumstances appear in the witness box. If prisoners in Ikey's day thus were under greater disadvantages than today, the dice were not completely loaded against them. It sometimes happened that, although a professional criminal could afford to employ a counsel to defend him, the prosecutor was unable to afford counsel to present the case against him.

The trials of prisoners indicted for felony were heard at assizes, or at sessions of oyer and terminer (Norman French for 'to hear and determine') and gaol delivery held at the Old Bailey. (The Central Criminal Court was not established until 1834, but the change in that year was mainly in name.) The Old Bailey served both the City of London and the county of Middlesex; offences which had occurred in the City were tried before a jury from

London, and those which had occurred in Middlesex before a jury drawn from the county. At the June sessions in 1810 Isaac Solomons and Joel Joseph appeared before a Middlesex jury. The evidence given at Bow Street was repeated. Thomas Dodd, the prosecutor, identified his pocket-book and said that he had lost it at the meeting in Palace Yard. John Vickery, the police officer, described the arrest of Solomons and Joseph and the search and discovery of the stolen property. John Preston, Vickery's assistant, corroborated his colleague's evidence and told of his own part in the arrest. William Ross, a bystander, testified to the truth of the statements of the two officers, and added the important piece of evidence that he had seen Solomons drop the pocket-book that Vickery picked up and that was later identified by Thomas Dodd. The two prisoners were then given their opportunity to explain these facts; although they could not give evidence on oath, they were allowed to address the jury from the dock. Joseph, who had been found with the stolen notes on him, told the court that he had found the pocket-book and had kept the notes 'intending to restore them to their owner'. Isaac Solomons's answer was that he had been at the meeting 'from curiosity alone' and that he was entirely innocent. The two prisoners could hardly have been surprised when the jury rejected these lame excuses and found them guilty. They had to wait a day or two to learn their fate—at that time sentences were not passed on prisoners individually at the end of their trial. All those who had been convicted during the sessions appeared again before the Recorder on the last day, when one by one sentence was passed upon them. On 14th June, 1810, Isaac Solomons and Joel Joseph received the maximum sentence for the crime of which they had been convicted: they were sentenced to be transported 'beyond the seas' for the term of their natural life.

The two prisoners returned to Newgate, where they had been lodged since their committal for trial on 19th April. Now that they had been sentenced to transportation, however, they would not be long detained in Newgate. That prison was primarily a place for those awaiting trial in London and Middlesex, or for convicted prisoners awaiting execution, although there were also bankrupts, lunatics, and others confined within its walls. The normal practice was that those sentenced to transportation, who were usually known simply as 'transports', were transferred to one of the hulks on the River Thames which served as prisons. The use of former warships for this purpose had begun after the American Revolution had made it impossible to dispose of convicts by sending them across the Atlantic. By Ikey's day there were a number of hulks, on the Thames and elsewhere, and it was by no means unusual for someone sentenced to transportation to spend his imprisonment in the hulks in England, probably serving about half of the original term. Prisoners would be taken from the hulks as ships became available to take them to Australia, and the people with longer sentences would normally be picked out to go overseas. However, age, health, and conduct on board the hulk, and perhaps other factors about which we are ignorant, affected the decision.

The hulks were moored near a dockyard or arsenal, and convicts were, for the most part, employed at work there—doing, it was said, 'everything the most laborious the Navy Board and Ordnance Department can find them to do'. They moved ballast out of and into ships, cleaned the ships, took up mooring chains, cleared mud from the docks, and moved timber around—the use of horses for this purpose had been discontinued. A strict account was kept of the work done by each gang and for every shilling's worth a convict performed, he was entitled to a penny. Each week he received only one-third of the amount which he had earned, the balance being carried forward until he was discharged; a man who had been six or seven years on board the hulks could have saved £10 or £12 by the time of his discharge.

When prisoners arrived at the hulks, whether from Newgate or from the various county gaols, they were immediately stripped and washed, and dressed in the convicts' coarse grey uniform. Precise details of the clothing they were given are known, for the account books were carefully preserved and are still available in the Public Record Office. When Joel Joseph and Isaac Solomons, on 10th July, 1810, joined the 400 convicts on board the hulk *Zealand* in the River Medway off Sheerness, they were each given one jacket, one waistcoat, one pair of breeches, one pair of stockings, two shirts, one handkerchief, one pair of shoes, one hat, one bed, two blankets, and one pair of irons. A pair of irons was placed on the legs of every convict in the hulk, but by good conduct they could obtain a lighter pair. It is sometimes suggested that money, as well as good conduct, would obtain a lighter pair of irons, and it may be for this reason that in the quarter beginning 1st October, 1810, Ikey was issued with another pair of irons. We do not know that they were lighter ones, but it was unusual for a new pair of irons to be issued to a convict so soon after his arrival; bribery may have been the explanation. Ikey also received during his second quarter on board the hulk another pair of stockings, another shirt, handkerchief, pair of shoes and a hat, and this comprehensive re-equipment may be evidence that he stood in good favour. An uncle of his is said to have been a slop-seller (seller of cheap clothing) in Chatham and this local connexion may have been useful to him.

After his second issue in the October quarter of 1810, however, Ikey did not do too well for a time. He got another shirt at the beginning of 1811, and a shirt, a handkerchief and pair of shoes in the July quarter that year. In the whole of 1812 all he received was one shirt. In 1813 he had a handkerchief and a pair of shoes in the January quarter, followed by a jacket, waistcoat, shirt and a pair of stockings in the April quarter, and another jacket, pair of stockings, pair of shoes, hat and handkerchief at the end of the year. Thereafter he did well: two jackets in 1814, one in 1815 and two in 1816; two waistcoats and two pairs of breeches in 1814 and again in 1815; ten pairs of shoes in twelve quarters in 1814–16, as well as six shirts and seven handkerchiefs and four more hats. In all, apart from his initial issue, he received seven jackets, six waistcoats, five pairs of breeches, seven pairs of stockings, fourteen pairs of shoes, eleven shirts, eleven hand-kerchiefs, six hats and four blankets, in the twenty-six quarters he was in the hulks. This seems a generous scale of issue, parti-cularly when one remembers the rags in which a large part of the population dressed at the time; yet Ikey was not treated particularly generously. In one quarter taken at random, 449 convicts (not including any new arrivals in the hulk) received between them 228 jackets, 204 waistcoats, 283 pairs of breeches, 295 pairs of stockings, 276 pairs of shoes, 295 shirts, 271 handkerchiefs, 204 hats and 126 blankets. That is to say, in that quarter there was an issue of each article to roughly half the convicts, except for blankets, received by about a quarter of them. Thus Ikey could have expected about 13 issues of each item during his 26 quarters in the hulks, apart from blankets, of which he could have expected 6 or 7. In most cases, therefore, Ikey got less than his share of what was going.

As well as their clothing, convicts were issued with bedding, either hammocks or flock beds, although some had merely sacking stuffed with straw. Each man had one or two blankets and a rug. In fine weather the bedding was brought on deck to be aired. It was examined on the first Monday of each month, and 'washed if necessary'. Clean straw was issued then. The convicts' sleeping quarters between decks were illuminated with lamps, and watchmen were appointed 'who every half-hour sing out "All's well"'.

The convicts on the hulks were roused at six in the morning and were allowed an hour in which to wash themselves, for which purpose soap and towels were provided. After breakfast the men went immediately on shore to work. They returned on board the hulk to have their dinner at twelve noon, for which an hour and a half was allowed. During this period convicts who were skilled tailors, shoemakers, etc., would earn money by doing odd jobs for their fellows. The afternoon working period followed this and the men were locked up in their quarters by eight p.m. Lights out was at ten p.m.

The convicts were divided into messes of six men for eating purposes. Each mess received daily 7 lb. 14 oz. of bread, and 9 pints of table-beer. Each morning a 'grout' of barley and oatmeal was served, 1 lb. 8 oz. to each mess, and a similar quantity was served either at midday dinner or as a supper allowance. On Sundays, Tuesdays, Thursdays and Saturdays, dinner for each mess consisted of 5 lb. 14½ oz. of beef; on Mondays, Wednesdays and Fridays it was 2 lb. 10 oz. of cheese. Such rations were, of course, quite good in comparison with what many poor people of the period had to content themselves with, but we have no means of knowing what quality of provisions was given to the convicts or whether they did in fact get the amounts that they were supposed to.

On discharge a convict was given a jacket and waistcoat, a pair of duck trousers or breeches, a pair of stockings, a pair of shoes, a shirt and a canvas hat—'all new'—and 10s. 6d. in money. Joel Joseph, Ikey's companion, was soon re-kitted, receiving jacket, waistcoat, breeches, shoes, hat, handkerchief, two shirts and two pairs of stockings. However, this was not because of his discharge—he had been selected for a draft for Australia. On 10th March, 1811, Joseph was taken from the *Zealand*, and on 12th May, he sailed in the *Admiral Gambier* for New South Wales, ending up as a publican in Sydney. Ikey was not included in the draft for the *Admiral Gambier*, and was to spend six years in the hulks without being sent overseas. Early in 1814 all the convicts in the *Zealand* were transferred to another hulk, the *Retribution*. Ikey remained in this hulk for a further two years or so, until he regained his freedom in rather peculiar circumstances.

Richard Gregory, a businessman who took an active interest in the policing of Spitalfields and who knew Ikey well, told a select committee of the House of Commons in 1828 'I was told . . . that an order came from the Secretary of State to discharge a prisoner of the name of Solomons for some offence, and in mistake the captain of the ship discharged Ikey Solomons, and he very artfully went and delivered himself up, as being discharged as the wrong person.' Ten years later, Edward Gibbon Wakefield, the founder of New Zealand and a writer on prison matters (with some authority—he had been imprisoned in Newgate for attempting to abduct an heiress), told a similar story. Solomons, he said, was released in error and his father told him to go down to the Home Office and explain—'The mistake will bring you a pardon'. It appears that these stories are, in substance, correct. We cannot be sure, but the following seems to be what happened.

On 4th June, 1816, the Home Office sent down to the *Retribution* a notification that the periods of transportation to be served by Solomons and three other convicts were to be reduced. This was quite a normal step. It is certainly easy to see why the sentences on the three other convicts were to be reduced. They were all over sixty years old and two of them had been ill for long periods. Between July, 1810, and December, 1815, Michael Gerain had spent 580 days in the hospital ship—or possibly more, for some of the records are missing; William Hall had, in the same period, spent 471 days in hospital. These two men had their sentences reduced to seven years, and this entitled them to immediate release, in view of the time that they had already spent in the hulks. They were released on 27th June, 1816. The sentences on Ikey Solomons and on the fourth man, Richard Hook, had been reduced to fourteen years, which left them still several years to serve. However, they were both released on 28th June, the day after Gerain and Hall. The simplest explanation is that some confusion arose between the two who were entitled to immediate release and the two who were not. It is thus not necessary to think of a confusion of names to explain Ikey's release, but a mistake of identity could have arisen. One Jonas Solomon was serving a sentence in *Retribution* at the time of Ikey's release, and this Jonas Solomon was given a free pardon and released later on in the year. It is, therefore, possible that the earlier pardon was intended for him and not for Ikey, but this would add another mistake to the one which was made when Hook and Solomons were released.

Thus the story that Isaac Solomons was released in error is true. It seems also that the story that he gave himself up to the authorities is equally true—he re-entered the hulk on 15th July, 1816. He had apparently kept his hulk uniform, for he had only a limited issue of clothing—and no irons. Whether in recognition of his having surrendered himself, or merely because an official mistake had been made in releasing him, he was granted a free pardon on 26th October, 1816, and released again on 31st October.

The hulk authorities had some difficulty in recording these

events in their register, which contains a careful notation of how each prisoner was disposed of. Whereas Richard Hook's entry ends 'Sentence commuted to fourteen years, pardoned 28th June 1816', Ikey's ends 'Sentence commuted to fourteen years, pardoned 31st October 1816'. The register thus avoids any reference to his release in June and his return to the hulk in July. We should not have been able to confirm this story about his release and reimprisonment had it not been for the scrupulous methods of the Treasury, as careful in those days as it is today. Every quarter the captain of each hulk had to account to the Treasury for the rations consumed on board and the stores issued, and he did this by sending in a nominal roll of every member of the crew and every convict, showing the number of days' rations issued to each one. It is from these accounts that we are able to establish that Ikey left the hulk in June and returned to it in July, and so are able to penetrate behind the bland entry against his name in the register and establish the facts. It is the ration returns that help us to understand how it was that on 31st October, 1816, Ikey Solomons left the hulk a free man.

c

Chapter Two

PICKPOCKETS AND POLICING

Although Isaac Solomons's passage through the courts and prisons of London after his arrest as a pickpocket in 1810 can be documented from the records, we cannot trace so accurately his activities before his career was abruptly checked. It is clear that Ikey and his companion, Joel Joseph, were expert and experienced pickpockets, for the victim of the crime did not notice the loss of his pocket-book at the time, but merely discovered later that it was missing. To steal a pocket-book without alarming its owner demanded skill, skill that could only be acquired by long practice. We do not know how Ikey got his training, but it is possible to draw on other material to provide a picture of the young pickpockets of London. It is also possible to learn something of Ikey's life as a pickpocket by considering the policing of his day, for there was a close relationship between detectives and pickpockets—one proof of Ikey's high standing in his craft is the ease with which John Vickery, the police officer, recognized him and his companion.

A good account of the apprenticeship which had to be served in order to become a skilled pickpocket is contained in the fourth volume of Henry Mayhew's *London Labour and London Poor*, published in 1861. A former pickpocket, talking about life in the 1840s, describes how, as a poor country boy without family or home, he slept with several other ragged boys under the arches of the Adelphi, off the Strand. This haunt was just by the Adelphi Stairs, a landing-stage for the ferry which carried people across the River Thames for a halfpenny each. As the passengers went up the steep hill from the river bank to the Strand, the boys would follow after them and steal their handkerchiefs. The new boy was eventually persuaded by his companions to take part in the thefts. They 'had been very kind to me, sharing what they got with me, but always asking why I did not try my hand, till at last I was ashamed to live any longer on the food they gave me without doing something for myself.' The new boy, Dick, had a special friend in one of the Adelphi boys, and 'Jo said to me, that when the next boat came in, if any man came out likely to carry a good handkerchief, he would let me have a chance at it. I recollect when the boat came in that evening: I think it was the last one, about nine o'clock. I saw an elderly gentleman step ashore, and a lady with him. They had a little dog, with a string attached to it, that they led along. Before Jo said anything to me, he had "fanned" the gentleman's pocket, i.e., had felt the pocket and knew there was a hand-kerchief. He whispered to me, "Now, Dick, have a try", and I went to the old gentleman's side, trembling all the time, and Jo standing close to me in the dark, and went with him up the steep hill of the Adelphi. He had just passed an apple-stall there, Jo still following us, encouraging me all the time, while the old gentleman was engaged with the little dog. I took out a green "kingsman" [handkerchief], next in value to a black silk hand-kerchief.' The gentleman did not notice that the handkerchief had gone and the boys went at once to the receiver who took their haul: 'Jo said to him, "there is Dick's first file, and you must give him a 'ray' for it," (one shilling and six pence). After a deal of pressing he got one shilling for it.'

Dick the Adelphi boy had had a harder start in life than Isaac Solomons, for Ikey had parents and a family and a home to return to. But his basic training in picking pockets was probably not very different. One of the accounts of his life published in 1830, the year of his greatest fame, says that Ikey started selling goods in the street at the age of nine—and implies that he was already selling stolen goods at that time. One of his brothers, the writer continues, was prosecuted for selling stolen goods but was acquitted, while the third was a respectable young man. However, this writer did not know as much as he claimed of Ikey's family, for he describes Ikey as the eldest of three survivors of a family of nine—but Ikey had a married sister and this, with the two brothers mentioned, would mean that four of the family survived their infancy. None the less, the author may not be far out when he says that Ikey, 'having initiated himself into the society of gamesters, prostitutes, *prigs* [thieves], and suchlike characters . . . found that the sharing of minor robberies were inadequate to his increasing wants'. Accordingly, he says, Ikey became active in planning robberies but was cautious enough usually to reserve for himself the role of look-out.

Another of the booklets about Ikey gives a slightly different version. From the age of eight, it says, Ikey, although nominally earning his living by selling oranges and lemons in the street, was in fact mainly interested in the profits he gained by giving false coin to his customers in their change—he was engaged by a gang of counterfeiters as one of their outlets. However, he soon grew out of this and, by the age of fourteen, says this writer, Ikey was a successful pickpocket, although he had also begun to act as a fence for the young thieves of his area.

Dick the Adelphi boy, according to his own story, was also a successful pickpocket; he claimed that he became one of the cleverest of the little band, 'never missing one boat coming in, and getting one or two handkerchiefs on each occasion'. Dick had learned the art of stealing from the pockets in the tails of the then fashionable tailcoats. However, after a few months his luck ran out and one of his victims caught him with a handkerchief in his hand. He was taken to Bow Street police station, and at his trial was sentenced to two months' imprisonment in Westminster Bridewell. It is possible that Ikey had a similar experience, although there is no record of it. Dick's arrest did not harm his career. He came out of prison in March, 1841, and found waiting for him two men who had seen him at work near the Adelphi Stairs. They asked him if he was willing to go with them, and when he replied that he was 'willing to go anywhere to better myself', they took him in a cab to their home in Flower-and-Dean Street, Whitechapel, a notorious haunt of criminals, and a street very familiar to Ikey Solomons, only a stone's throw from Gravel Lane. Dick was recruited into a gang of expert pickpockets, one of the skilled groups which did not content itself with mere handkerchiefs but went for the more difficult purses and wallets. A single pickpocket could seldom be successful at such targets. He needed others, to shield him from passers-by who might otherwise see what was happening, to jostle the victim to give him the opportunity of stealing, and to take the booty from him as soon as it was stolen so that, if the alarm was raised, nothing would be found on anyone near enough to be accused. The actual thief was often a boy, like the lad from the Adelphi. His companions had recruited him to take the place of another boy, who had just been arrested and transported to Australia, leaving the gang without a vital member.

Dick's companions were a gang who concentrated on picking ladies' pockets, and for two or three days he was carefully rehearsed in this, with the assistance of a woman member of the gang. 'They had stood against me in the room while Emily walked to and fro, and I had practised on her pocket by taking out sometimes a lady's clasp purse, termed a "porte monnaie", and other articles out of her pocket.' Then the group were ready to go out to steal. 'It was on a Saturday, in company with three men, I set out on an excursion from Flower-and-Dean Street along Cheapside. They were young men, from nineteen to twenty-five years of age, dressed in fashionable style. I was clothed in the suit given me when I came out of prison, a beaver-hat, a little surtout-coat, and trousers, both of black cloth, and a black silk necktie and collar, dressed as a gentleman's son.' Eventually the group saw a likely-looking prospect. 'One walked in front of me, one on my right hand, and the other in the rear, and I had the lady on my left hand. I immediately "fanned" her (felt her pocket) as she stopped to look in at a hosier's window, when I took her purse and gave it to one of them.' The group found a pound or two in the purse, and, as was the usual practice, promptly threw away everything but the money, to avoid having compromising evidence on them. They got four more purses that afternoon, and were home by 5 p.m. 'I recollect how they praised me afterwards that night at home for my cleverness.' A few days later they went out again, and for two days' work the gang earned £19 each. 'They always take care to allow the boy to see what is in the purse, and to give him his proper share equal with the others, because he is their sole support. If they should lose him they would be unable to do anything till they got another.'

Ikey worked with a gang in the same way, though not from Flower-and-Dean Street. He had had to leave his home area, for he had become too well known to the City police. On at least one occasion he escaped prosecution by bribery alone. He moved to the West End and became a member of a gang there. He is said to have offended against the code which Dick mentions and was detected by his colleagues keeping too much of his proceeds for himself. In consequence he was shunned by the others and had to work without the protection of a large gang. As we have seen, he was working with only one companion when he was caught—if he had had the usual four or five, the property would have been far away before Vickery reached the pair who had taken it, and a search would not have produced anything incriminating.

Of course, even a large gang of pickpockets could not always prevent the arrest of the actual thief, as Dick the Adelphi boy explained. 'I was caught in Fleet Street, and they had no means of getting me away, though they tried all they could to secure my escape. They could not do it without exposing themselves to too much suspicion.' The offence having been committed in the City of London, Dick had to serve his sentence of three months' imprisonment in the Bridewell in Blackfriars. He was not neglected whilst there: 'During my imprisonment I did not live on the prison diet, but was kept on good rations supplied to me through the kindness of my comrades out of doors bribing the turnkeys. I had tea of a morning, bread and butter, and often cold meat. Meat and all kinds of pastry was sent to me from a cook-shop outside, and I was allowed to sit up later than other prisoners. During the time I was in prison for these three months I learned to smoke, as cigars were introduced to me.'

Dick stayed with his first gang of friends for a couple of years or so, through a couple of imprisonments, but eventually left them owing to a dispute about property which had disappeared whilst he was in prison. 'They pretended it was laid out in my defence, which I knew was only a pretext.' After a further term of imprisonment, Dick began to work on his own, as Ikey Solomons did—by this time, Dick was about fifteen years old. His principal target was gentlemen's watches or tiepins. 'I looked out for crowds at fairs, at fires, and on any occasion where there was a gathering of people, as at this time I generally confined myself to watches, and pins from men. I was not so lucky then, and barely kept myself in respectability. My woman was very extravagant, and swallowed up all I could make.'

For the next few years Dick was one of the leading pickpockets of London, sometimes working with the swell mob, the high-class pickpockets who worked on ladies' purses. With his friends he went to the gathering of the Chartists on Kennington Common at the time of the presentation of the People's Charter in April, 1848. This event was heralded as the approach of revolution and it so alarmed middle-class London that a large number of special constables was sworn in, including Louis Napoleon, nephew of the great Emperor and the future Napoleon III. However, politically the presentation of the Charter proved a damp squib: by agreement with the police it was taken to Westminster in a hansom cab, while the crowds remained south of the river at Kennington. A crowd was a target for pickpockets, whatever the motive for its meeting, and Dick did well. 'I went to this gathering on 10th April, 1848, along with three men. I took several ladies' purses there, amounting to three pounds or four pounds, when we saw a gentleman place a pocket-book in the tail of his coat. Though I had done nothing at the tail for a long time, it was too great a temptation, and I immediately seized it. There was a bundle of bank-notes in it—seven ten-pound notes, two for twenty pounds, and five five-pound notes. We got from the fence or receiver four pounds ten shillings for each of the five pounds, eight pounds ten shillings for the tens, and eighteen pounds for the twenty pound notes. The same afternoon I took a purse in Trafalgar Square with about 18 sovereigns in it.'

Dick's account of his activities could, to some extent, be that of Ikey Solomons. The crimes that the two committed were very much the same, and their experiences were similar. Like Ikey, Dick was well known to the police. 'We were frequently watched by the police and detectives, who followed us back, and were often in the same places of amusement with us. We knew them as well as they knew us, and often eluded them. Their following us has often been the means of our doing nothing on many of these occasions, as we knew their eye was upon us.' Like Ikey, Dick eventually turned to different forms of crime and different ways of earning a living, and it seems that picking pockets was a crime for younger men.

A few years before Dick commenced his career, a twenty-three-year-old named Nelson had the reputation of being the most expert pickpocket in London. Like others of the swell mob he had the manners of a gentleman and dressed accordingly. Not only did this enable him to mix in the crowd where the greatest booty was to be obtained, but it also meant that he had a greater chance of escape should suspicion be thrown upon him. On one occasion, in St James's Street, Nelson was accused by a gentleman of stealing his purse, containing nine sovereigns. Nelson had indeed taken the purse but had passed it away rapidly to another of his gang, so that nothing was found on him. Nelson expressed the greatest indignation that a gentleman of his family and respectability should even be suspected of theft, and the victim was apologizing for his mistake, when a police superintendent who knew Nelson arrived and ordered a more careful search. Although they did not find the purse which had just been stolen, they did find someone else's purse, and Nelson ended up in the House of Correction. This was just one of many visits to prison, but his short spells in gaol did not prevent Nelson from making a regular living as a criminal, often earning £10 a day and on one occasion, it was said, stealing £25 along Piccadilly between the hours of 1 p.m. and 6 p.m. Nelson spent most of his time in the fashionable streets of London—Piccadilly, Bond Street, St. James's Street and Regent Street. He would wait outside the high-class shops of the neighbourhood, watching to see where men put their purses after making a purchase. Then he or his young confederates would take an opportunity to pick the pocket. Nelson had started in the trade as a youngster in his early 'teens, and had had ten years of experience at the time of which we are speaking.

It was in the course of acquiring the experience necessary to become a member of the swell mob that a pickpocket became known to the detectives of London. Although the Metropolitan Police had not been introduced by Robert Peel when Ikey Solomons was at work—it was not formed until 1829—criminals did not have it all their own way and there was a policing system which, for all its faults, was not completely ineffective. There were some fifty detectives in the London area, operating from Bow Street and other police offices. There were patrol forces, run from the Bow Street Office, some in uniform and some in plain clothes. There were parish watchmen, some of them of little value but others active and resolute. The City of London had its own detectives, patrols and watchmen, organized separately from those of the rest of the metropolis.

The most famous of the detectives of London were those who were known as the Bow Street Runners: the official title of these men was 'police officer'. The post had originated in the days of Henry Fielding, Bow Street magistrate in the years 1748–54. When Fielding took up his office, the only help a magistrate could get in the detection of crime came from the parish constables or their deputies (a frail reed, as we shall see in subsequent paragraphs) or from the thief-takers, who were a dangerous weapon to use. The thief-takers were individuals who had taken upon themselves the investigation of crime, their motive being the rewards which were paid by various official bodies or by the victims of crime for the conviction of offenders. These men were not appointed by any public authority and were responsible to no one; they acted purely for their own profit. The thief-takers had acquired an evil reputation. Some of them emulated the great Jonathan Wild, the master-criminal of London in the years 1715–25, and were criminals themselves as well as prosecuting others. Even if they did not actually steal themselves, they were

sometimes the originators of much of the crime that they prosecuted, for it was obviously easier to catch a thief if you had
encouraged him and assisted him to commit his crime in the
first place.

This necessity of relying on weak or corrupt assistants was not
satisfactory to Henry Fielding. He has been described as the
founder of London's modern police system. He sought honest
men to help in the active investigation of crime and gathered
around him a small group of men, whom he employed in
detecting cases reported to him. Inspired by Fielding's example
and encouragement, they continued to act after they had served
their normal term of office as parish constable. This tiny band
of men, who received a very small salary, became the first paid
and officially appointed detectives of London. They were for a
time called 'Mr. Fielding's People', but eventually became known
as the Bow Street Runners. By Ikey Solomons's day, there were
eight police officers attached to the Bow Street Office. John
Vickery, who arrested Ikey in 1810, was promoted to the Bow
Street Office a year or so later, after eleven years' experience as
a police officer, and became one of the top half-dozen detectives
of London. At the time he arrested Ikey he was serving at one
of the police offices created in 1792, when the system begun by
Henry Fielding had been extended and seven more police offices
set up on the model of Bow Street.

A police office was a place which was a magistrates' court as
we know it today, but much more besides. The magistrates of
the early nineteenth century had three responsibilities in the
criminal field, whereas their modern counterparts have only one.
The responsibility that has been retained is that of acting in a
judicial capacity, either disposing of minor cases or making an
initial investigation into more serious charges before committing
the accused for trial at a higher court, together with the duty of
issuing warrants and summonses, etc. The two responsibilities
which magistrates have shed have been passed on to senior police
officers: in former times magistrates were responsible for the
maintenance of public order and for the investigation of crime.
These were no light duties, as a further examination will show.

All the magistrates of the country had a responsibility as the guardians of public order. When any disorder threatened in the streets they were expected to give instructions for the intervention of the forces of law and order and, moreover, to lead them in person. When there was a threat of riots, when an unlawful assembly had to be dispersed, when processions or other public events caused large crowds to gather in the streets, or even when officers made raids on gaming houses or coiners' workplaces if the offence was more than usually serious, the magistrates went with the constables who were to enforce their orders. However, in the London area it was the stipendiary magistrates, rather than the unpaid justices of the peace, to whom people turned on these occasions. So great was the reputation of the stipendiaries that, according to one foreign writer, they had been seen 'in the most critical circumstances to disperse assemblies by their presence alone'.

We are, however, more interested in the magistrates' role as the men in charge of criminal investigations: the stipendiaries had a responsibility for supervising the activities of the police officers, the salaried detectives attached to their court. They directed the investigation of crimes reported to them, in something of the manner of an American district attorney or a French *juge d'instruction*. It was, in general, the magistrates who decided which cases should be investigated and by whom, and they would often take a close personal interest, calling for the statements of people whom they thought to have something useful to say and generally keeping a careful eye on what was done. The system of private prosecutions of course affected the matter. A case was unlikely to be investigated with great vigour if there was little chance of a reward for the return of the stolen property or at least a contribution towards the costs of enquiry, unless there were some special features which caused the magistrates to insist on investigation. In the ordinary course of events, victims of crime would, if they felt it worth their while and if they could afford to bear the costs even if no goods were returned to them, apply to the magistrates for the assistance of one of the police officers. When, many years after his arrest in 1810, Ikey Solomons

appeared in court as a receiver of stolen goods, his fate was due
to action of this sort. One Charles Strachan, who figured pro-
minently in the later stages of Ikey's career, in pursuit of some
stolen watches, had a long interview with John Hardwick, a
magistrate of the Lambeth Street Office. As a result of this
conversation James Lea, a Lambeth Street officer, was put on
Ikey's trail and ultimately caught him.

The system of depending so heavily on rewards from the
victims of crime had its risks, although the magistrates did their
best to prevent undesirable consequences. 'If any Officer',
resolved the magistrates of the Hatton Garden Office in 1813,
'shall presume to demand any reward as the price of doing his
duty, from any person or persons whatsoever' he should immediately be suspended, without pay, and discharged if he did
not give a satisfactory explanation of his conduct. Another
resolution provided that: 'No Officer shall upon any pretence go
above five miles from the Metropolis upon any duty, without the
consent and directions of some one or more of the Magistrates.'
Two other regulations show the attempt of the magistrates to
control the activities of their men: 'No business shall be postponed
to the evening, that can be done in a morning, unless by order of
the Magistrate of the day. . . . The Officers . . . shall within
twenty-four hours next after they make a seizure of goods or
property of any description whatever, deliver the particulars
thereof in writing to one of the Clerks, in order that entry of the
same may be made forthwith in the book provided for that
purpose.' In most cases the police officers assigned to a particular
crime would investigate it entirely on their own, but the magistrates retained a general right, and duty, to keep an eye on their
doings. When the new offices were established in 1792, half a
dozen police officers, detectives like their comrades at Bow Street,
were appointed at each of them. John Vickery served at Worship
Street, in East London. The detectives of each office investigated
on behalf of their magistrates crimes committed in the area of
London assigned to the court.

The City of London, which was not within the jurisdiction of
any of the police offices, eventually acquired its own detectives,

responsible to its own court at the Mansion House. Two brothers
named Forrester were engaged by the City authorities, John in
1817 and Daniel in 1821, and for many years they ran a semi-
official detective agency from their office near the Justice Rooms
of the Mansion House. They continued to be employed until
1857, although the Bow Street Runners and the other police
officers of this old style were made redundant by the reorganiza-
tion of the Metropolitan Police and of the police courts in 1839.
The Forrester brothers were more highly paid than the Bow
Street Runners: they received £78 a year, and a rent-free office
as well. From the office they ran their private detective agency,
for like the Runners they did not regard themselves as bound to
devote all their time to their official duties.

Despite the high reputation of the Forrester brothers, the Bow
Street Runners were the leading detectives of London. Because
of the earlier origin of their office, they were not confined to
investigation of crimes in the area immediately around Bow
Street but had a general roving brief over the whole of the
metropolis. Indeed, Bow Street officers would at times go elsewhere in the country. John Vickery, after his transfer to Bow
Street, often left London. For example, on one occasion he spent
a fortnight in Gloucestershire at the request—and expense—of a
Colonel Berkeley. Officers would go abroad if necessary. However, they were only prepared to travel away from London if
suitable guarantees were forthcoming that their expenses would
be repaid.

Charles Dickens rather makes fun of the Bow Street Runners
in *Oliver Twist*, in which Blathers and Duff (significant names)
are rapidly able to establish to their own satisfaction who has
been responsible for the attempted burglary at Chertsey; they
each have a different theory, and they are both wrong. There is,
however, ample evidence that the Runners were often much
more successful than this, and the detectives were able and
experienced men, often with an uncanny knowledge of the pickpockets of the day. One of the most famous of the Bow Street
Runners was John Townsend. He was first appointed to the
Office in the early 1780s, before Ikey was born, but was still active

in 1816, when Ikey was released from the hulks. Townsend had
the task of protecting the King and the Prince Regent on public
occasions, and was employed by the Bank of England on 'dividend
days', when large sums were paid out in cash. He and another
officer went to the Bank on forty such days a year to look out
for pickpockets, each receiving a guinea a day in addition to his
ordinary pay. Townsend was often engaged to appear at fashionable parties; when the invitation bore the words 'Mr. Townsend
will attend', ladies could wear expensive jewellery and men carry
elaborate snuff boxes with a greater feeling of security, for when
Townsend attended the swell mob did not. As we have seen,
it was a police officer's knowledge of regular pickpockets which
was Ikey Solomons's undoing. If John Vickery had not recognized
Ikey and his companion when he saw them on 17th April,
1810, he would have had no reason to follow them as they left
the crowd in New Palace Yard and no reason to seize them, and
thus would not have found the stolen property on them.

Although the system had its successes, it undoubtedly had its
imperfections. One major weakness was that the officers could
not live on their salary of a guinea a week; this fairly small
amount was regarded merely as a retainer. Their main source of
income was the rewards for the successful prosecution of offenders
and for the return of the stolen property. The rewards for the
prosecution of offenders could come from official funds, because
sizeable sums, usually £40, were payable on the conviction of
certain types of offender. However, as several people might have
to share in the £40 paid on conviction of one burglar, the
officers could not expect too much from this source. Moreover,
they did not always get the reward when they expected it. John
Vickery told a select committee of the House of Commons of
a case in which a man named Asker had been indicted for burglary
in the house of the clerk of 'Mr. Wesley's chapel in the City-
road'. The house had been raided on a Sunday evening while
the clerk was at chapel. Asker was, in due course, convicted, but
only of stealing in a dwelling-house. As usual, Vickery received
a few shillings to pass on to the prosecutor to help cover his
expenses.

'He said, "Mr. Vickery, there is a reward attached to this, as well as this, I suppose?"—"No, Sir, there is not, for the Jury have got rid of the burglary, and there is no reward for this man's conviction" . . . "God bless me! What can be the reason?" —"Why, Sir, that you have neglected to state before the Jury, that you had been reading by candle-light, prior to your going out to evening service, and on that account we did not prove the burglary." "God bless my soul! You ought to have told me that . . . for this will not half pay my expenses for attending here." '

The prosecutor thus learned the hard way the rule of law that burglary could only be committed at night. As an essential ingredient of the burglary charge had not been proved, the prosecutor and Vickery lost the £40 reward. Vickery knew that if he had warned the prosecutor he would have added the vital words, and 'I have no doubt,' he said, 'the Jury would have convicted him of burglary, but I never suggest these things to witnesses'. Vickery said that he himself had never received as much as £20 a year from these rewards—'I speak of the rewards under the Act of Parliament, I do not include those offered by advertisement by parties injured'—in any of his five years at Bow Street (where rewards would be more plentiful than at the other offices). He went on to say that he did not believe that any of 'the six or seven principal officers at Bow Street' ever made as much as £40 a year from this source.

Another source of income to police officers and prosecutors was what was called a Tyburn ticket. Issued to those who had successfully prosecuted certain types of offender, the Tyburn ticket was a certificate of exemption from serving a parish office in the parish where the crime was committed. There were a number of unpaid parish offices which householders were required to hold for a year as their turn came round, and which brought unpleasant and time-consuming duties to the unwilling holder of the post. People were often prepared to pay a fine to the parish rather than serve the office, or to hire someone as deputy in their place. As the Tyburn ticket represented another means of excusing oneself from parish office, a police officer to whom one was issued was able to sell it to a parishioner of the place concerned.

John Vickery did not attach much importance to Tyburn tickets. 'The Tyburn-tickets in some parishes are at present of some trifling value, in others they are of no value whatever. . . . In the generality of parishes at present it is of no value; for instead of the officers wishing to be out of office, they are all trying, for some reason or other, to get into office, and that makes them of no value.' However, more precise details were given by his colleague John Townsend. He had sold Tyburn tickets 'as low as £12', while the most valuable tickets were those for the parish of St. Paul, Covent Garden, 'where it is worth £25; for the constable of the parish must sit up, I think, one night out of three; and whoever is hit upon as parochial constable says, "this is a hard thing, and therefore I will buy myself off." ' On the other hand, a ticket in St. George's, Hanover Square, was virtually worthless because of the wealth and public-spiritedness of the inhabitants: 'the people are of so much consequence that they will serve themselves.'

This whole system of rewards was regarded by the people of the day as unsatisfactory, for it led the police officers to direct their attention only to crimes which would earn them money. Still worse, it tempted the officers to ignore youngsters who committed lesser crimes, or rather to watch them until they had committed something which made it worth their while arresting them—until they 'weighed £40', as the cant phrase had it. Some officers, it was said, even went so far as to persuade youngsters into the commission of crime, in order to be able to arrest them later. Vickery said 'I have never waited to see a party commit an offence; but that I would take him in the act of doing it, rather than when the act was done.' Indeed, Townsend told the select committee of a case in which Vickery had warned the Secretary of the Post Office of an attempted crime: 'the Receiver General's Office was to be robbed; the very keys were all made, and . . . they only waited for a very large sum' to be left overnight. Vickery's warning ended the affair without the plan being put into operation and this would normally have meant that he received no reward, although in this case a more reasonable attitude seems to have prevailed. In many other cases, it is clear, officers found that, instead of preventing crime, it was more profitable to let criminals carry out their plans and then try to seize them and recover the stolen property. It was probably rare for officers actually to promote crime but the system was likely to make them reluctant to intervene too soon.

A further unsatisfactory feature of the system was that the interest of the victim of the crime was primarily in the return of the stolen property rather than the conviction of the thief, and this led police officers into temptation. They were often invited to act as intermediary between the thief and the victim for the return of the stolen property for a proportion of its value, with no questions asked and no attempt to apprehend the criminal. This was, of course, illegal and had been so for a hundred years or more, since the days of Jonathan Wild. None the less, it was often done and there is ample evidence that the practice existed on a considerable scale.

Some police officers, it is said, acquired considerable fortunes; Townsend is said to have amassed £20,000 and his colleague John Sayer £30,000, although there is no proof of this. Vickery made it clear in 1816 that he was a man of means: suggesting to the select committee that there should be pensions for retired police officers, he added, 'I am not speaking for myself, for perhaps I may never want it, but I am speaking on behalf of men who will want it; for . . . many of the officers hardly receive more reward for their service than is just enough to enable them to live without becoming thieves.' It is probably true that only a few of the more famous detectives earned large sums of money, and most of the police officers doubtless had little to compensate them for the dangers of their life—Vickery himself was laid up for a few months after an attack on him by three men in December, 1813.

It was the police officers who were the principal enemies of Ikey and his fellows, but they were not able entirely to ignore the preventive patrols. Although all the police offices of the metropolis had detectives, it was only the Bow Street Office which

D

had preventive patrols. Two of them were in existence when Ikey started his operations, and two more had been created before he finally left London for good. The oldest established of the four forces was the Foot Patrol, placed on an organized basis around the year 1780. Its fifty or sixty members, in plain clothes, patrolled the streets of the central part of the town (except the City of London itself). It was purely a night force, operating from dusk until about 1 a.m. Men who had served in the army and navy were given preference for employment in the Foot Patrol, provided that they were below the age limit of thirty-five; the minimum height was five feet five inches. The ordinary members of the patrol were paid two shillings and sixpence a night, and the conductors, the men in charge of each small party, five shillings. Every man carried a truncheon and a cutlass, and some had pistols as well. Apart from their regular duty at night, they were sometimes employed for additional duties during the day—one member of the patrol who was at the Westminster meeting in 1810 assisted Vickery in apprehending Solomons and Joseph.

The second of the Bow Street Patrols was the Horse Patrol, established in 1805 to provide protection against highwaymen for travellers on the main roads around London. The members of the patrol rode up and down their assigned stretch of road, armed to the teeth and calling out 'Bow Street Patrol' in a loud voice as they approached travellers. They did not always advertise their presence in this way, however, and John Pearson, writing in 1827, described how they would be found 'skulking about behind trees in ambush . . . nor do you know where they are until you are absolutely under their horses' noses; hence these men prevent many robberies and murders'. The Horse Patrol was a uniformed force, wearing a blue coat and trousers and a scarlet waistcoat; the latter gained for its members the nickname of 'robin redbreast'.

The Bow Street Patrols were augmented in 1821, when the Foot Patrol was concentrated within a smaller area in the centre of the town, because of anxiety about an increase in the number of robberies there. This left a gap between the Foot and the

Horse Patrol, and to fill it there was created a new body with the paradoxical name of the Dismounted Horse Patrol. It was given that name because it was part of the Horse Patrol establishment and operated broadly in the same manner, with men patrolling up and down the main roads; however, because they operated within the built-up area, they were on foot. The Horse Patrol and the Dismounted Horse Patrol were both night forces like the Foot Patrol; it was only in 1822 that the Bow Street Office acquired an organized body to patrol during the day. In that year, a small Day Patrol was established, to cover the central part of the town. It was only a tiny body—some thirty men—but it seems to have been effective as an addition to the forces of law and order.

None of these forces operated in the City of London itself. The City had its own patrols. Twelve day patrols covered the four divisions of the City—'and a very active body of men they are', said their supervisor in 1816—and eight night patrols came on at 9 p.m. in the summer and 6 p.m. in the winter. The City's Upper and Under Marshal, salaried permanent officers, had a general oversight of its police.

The most numerous law enforcement body in the London area in Ikey's day does not really demand great attention from us, for it certainly did not interfere with his operations as a pickpocket, nor was it likely to have much impact on his subsequent career as a receiver. There were some 5,000 constables and watchmen in the metropolis, representatives of the policing system bequeathed by the Middle Ages to subsequent centuries. In the Middle Ages there had developed a system by which each parish had its constables. This was one of the parish offices referred to earlier, an unpaid and usually unwanted post which, particularly in London, brought heavy and unpleasant duties with it. The parish constable was the official representative of law and order in his parish. If riot or disorder developed, the constable was supposed to attend the scene, bearing his staff of office—the symbol of royal authority, and the equivalent of a warrant-card in a non-literate age—to quell the disturbance. He was responsible for seeing that public houses were properly conducted and that no tippling (drinking to the point of drunkenness) was permitted. He was responsible for the serving of summonses and the execution of warrants, for the suppression of begging and the removal of vagrants. These duties were all to be done without salary, although certain fees were payable on performance of some of them. In the urban parishes, the constable had additional duties in relation to the parochial night watch.

In the parishes of London, there would often be four or five constables appointed for each year, one of whom was to do duty each night. A man might thus be required to be constable of the night once every four or five nights, as his turn came round. The constable of the night was supposed to attend at the parish watch-house in the evening, when the night watch came on duty, to call the roll of watchmen and to inspect them as they went out to their posts. He was supposed to patrol the parish once or twice during the night, to see that the watchmen were awake, and in the meantime to remain at the watchhouse to receive the charges when prisoners were brought in by the watchmen. He was to call over the roll again when the watchmen returned to the watchhouse as they went off duty in the morning.

Many of those upon whom the duty of constable was thrust must have performed it unwillingly and must have done as little as possible. As Vickery put it, 'if he hears that one of his neighbours is robbed, he won't wag out of his own shop till the Magistrate sends for him, and obliges him to do his duty.' As we saw earlier, the Tyburn ticket given as a reward for prosecuting certain offenders gave exemption from parish offices, and to earn or buy one was thus a way to get out of the duties. Money could absolve men from duty in another way, for some people paid deputies to do the work for them. John Vickery said in 1816, 'if a decent tradesman, or respectable inhabitant, is called upon to serve the office of parish-constable, he is indifferent to the performance of its duties, and he considers the office in some respects as an office of disgrace, and to avoid it he will give a man two or three guineas to perform the duties.' Obviously, those who looked for a deputy in this way looked not for the best man to do the job but for the cheapest substitute they could find, and the parish could therefore not expect to have the job done well. However, the custom did grow up of certain people serving as deputy constable for year after year, being paid by one parishioner after another as their turn came round. Although this meant that the duties of parish constable were not discharged by the substantial householders upon whom they were supposed to fall but by people of lesser respectability, the system of semi-permanent deputies did have some advantages. A continuity was developed in this way which might well have had some benefit to the parish.

There was another officer who could make up for some of the deficiencies of the constable of the parish. Most urban parishes, especially in London, employed a number of beadles, minor officials who were engaged on a permanent basis and paid a salary from parish funds. During the day, the beadle's principal concern was with the poor law—it was in this capacity that Mr. Bumble had his encounters with Oliver Twist. In the same way as the constables, the beadles would take it in turn to do duty as beadle of the night, and, being salaried officers, they were expected to attend without fail. Whether or not the constable of the night attended, it was the beadle on whom fell the principal responsibility of checking the watchmen on and off duty. Whether or not the constable of the night accompanied him, the beadle would go round the parish once or twice during the night, often reporting watchmen as being asleep or absent from their posts.

In the original medieval system, the post of watchman had been held by householders, on the same unpaid and compulsory basis as that by which the post of parish constable was filled. Just as someone was constable for the year as his turn came round, so he was watchman for the night as his turn came round for that duty. The householders in this original system watched over their own street and may well, at first, have been reasonably conscientious. We can imagine that very early in the life of the system the post of watchmen was filled not by the householder but by his son or apprentice, and we can imagine also that often he paid someone a few pence to do the duty. Eventually, however,

the system became debased, and householders would pay the
parish constable or the parish beadle a small sum, and from the
money thus collected a few watchmen were appointed for the
whole of the area. This was a purely unofficial arrangement,
however, and there was no means of checking what use was
made of the money collected. The arrangement had proved so
unsatisfactory that long before Ikey Solomons's day it had been
swept away. From 1735 there spread over most of the metropolis
a system which, in principle, was the same as that which we
know today. In many of the parishes of the London area, householders were required to pay a watch-rate, from the proceeds
of which salaried watchmen were employed, permanent public
officials subject to the control of the vestry of the parish or some
other publicly appointed ruling body.

Parish watches in the early nineteenth century varied considerably in quality. The best of them were extremely efficient
forces, with active officers ensuring that the watchmen remained
alert and did their duty. For example, in 1810 the parish of St.
George's, Hanover Square, one of the pioneers of the new system
of watching, had a night watch consisting of eighty-seven
watchmen, supervised by ten patrolling watchmen whose duty
was to go round parts of the parish checking on the other men,
under the supervision of the beadle of the night. There were six
beadles, so that each man did duty as beadle of the night seven
times in six weeks. By 1823 the number of watchmen had risen
to a hundred, and there were now fourteen patrolling watchmen.
In that year, moreover, the vestry decided to introduce a further
great improvement. During the four winter months of November,
December, January, and February, it resolved, 'There shall be
employed an additional number of twelve patrolling, two
supernumary patrolling and one hundred watchmen in order that
one of the sets of patrolling, supernumerary patrolling and
watchmen may be on duty from dusk until eleven or twelve
o'clock, and the other set from that time until seven a.m.' This
wealthy parish had clearly provided itself with an efficient watch
force. However, not all the parishes of London were so active.
Indeed, there were still some places where there was no watch-

rate and where the old system was still employed: householders made a small and unofficial payment to some parish official to be rid of the duty of watching in person. The parishes with the worst watch employed only a few old men, who would otherwise be a charge on the parish poor rate and who were, as it was said, employed by the parish to sleep in the open air. Even where there was an efficient parish watch, of course, some of its value was lost because of the smallness of the area over which it was operating and because of the existence of the other parishes where there was no efficient force. It was this unevenness of the policing of London which was one of the justifications for Robert Peel's reform of 1829. An act of that year swept away the network of parish forces and introduced the Metropolitan Police —but Ikey Solomons had lost interest in the policing of London by that time.

Chapter Three

THE GREAT IKEY SOLOMONS

After his fortunate release from the hulks in 1816 Ikey Solomons disappears from view for ten years. One story about him says that he spent some years working as a barker for his uncle, the Chatham slop-seller. Most of the accounts of his life agree that he turned to receiving stolen goods on his release, and this seems likely enough. Richard Gregory, a Spitalfields businessman who was active in running the night watch, said that Ikey went to live in his parish after his release and 'the moment he came into Spitalfields he left off thieving'. It is indeed unlikely that Ikey would have returned to his old trade of picking pockets. He would have had to learn the art again after his six years' confinement, and the work he had had to do in the hulks would have made him lose his delicacy of touch. Moreover, picking pockets was a boy's trade rather than a man's, although there were some adult pickpockets. In any event, we know that by 1826 Ikey had built up a flourishing connection as a receiver of stolen goods and it is possible that he turned to this trade immediately he was released from the hulks.

The hack writers of Ikey's day did their best, in the pamphlets about him published at the height of his fame, to fill in the ten-year blank in his life, between release from the hulks and the exposure of his lucrative receiving business With no worry about libel actions or any problems of contempt of court, and with few inhibitions about supplementing what they knew with what they thought might seem plausible, the writers told lurid stories about our hero. It is hardly possible that Ikey really committed all the infamies of which they accused him, but amongst the imaginings and exaggerations there is probably some truth.

These accounts of Ikey's life are certainly not dull. One had
the enticing title 'Only Correct Edition! The Life and Exploits
of Ikey Solomons, Swindler, forger, fencer, and brothel-keeper.
With accounts of flash and dress houses, flash girls and Coves of
the Watch, now on Town; With instructions how to guard
against Hypocritical Villains, and the lures of abandoned Females.
Also, particulars of Mrs. Ikey Solomons, and the Gang who
infested London for Nineteen Years'. This account is said to be
by Moses Hebron, 'formerly a Jewish Rabbi, but now a Christian.'
It says that Ikey did not receive any money from his father when
it was time for him to think of earning his own living, and that
he started in trade on his own resources, or rather those of his
wife. Ikey, according to this author, 'married his wife from the
bar of the "Blue Anchor" in Petticoat-Lane, a low public-house'
and 'got money' with her. Mrs. Solomons later described her
father as a coachmaster, the owner of an establishment where
coaches were let out on hire, and it is therefore quite likely that
she was given a dowry of some sort. With the money obtained
in this way, the author says, Ikey opened a clothes shop. However,
he does not think that Ikey long remained in honest ways and
goes on to accuse him of all sorts of villainy. Ikey, he says, had a
'prime and regular' dress-house—a brothel where the prostitutes
were supplied with their clothing by the brothel-keeper as well
as being boarded and lodged by him—in Angel-Court, Strand,
where the 'Misses Sparkes, Cruttwell, Jemina Mordaunt, Singing
Sal, Cherry Bounce and others, all eminent in their vocation',
lived and worked. Ikey, says the author, used this house for his
business of receiving stolen goods as well, but he had to shut
it eventually on an order of the Bow Street magistrates 'though
he used to boast that one half of the officers were in his pay, as
the other half wanted to be'. Ikey, he claims, also used to lend
money on bonds to needy young gentlemen, whose fathers
would in due course meet their sons' obligations rather than allow
publication of the facts and thus bring discredit on the family.
In sixteen lines, then, the author has accused Ikey of being a
brothel-keeper and a fence, of suborning police officers and of
money-lending under suspicious circumstances and by unfair

practices. We can hardly believe what he says. Although the account of Ikey's alleged brothel is certainly circumstantial enough in its terms, one would be happier if dates were given when all these activities were supposed to have taken place.

The author tells at greater length a story of the association which he claims existed between Solomons and a banker named John King, who married the widow of the second Earl of Lanesborough. A man named John King certainly did marry the widow, Jane, the only daughter of the first Earl of Belvedere. She was born in 1737, married Lord Lanesborough in 1754 and was widowed in 1779; she died in 1828. However, no banker of the name of King is listed in the thorough survey which exists of the private bankers of London of the eighteenth and nineteenth centuries, and this must cast considerable doubt on the story. According to the author, however, King's connection with the higher classes of London society gave him an advantage in his business; he was thereafter often approached for loans by impecunious young noblemen. King and Solomons combined to take advantage of these rash young men. The borrowers would put their names to bills of exchange binding them to pay sums of money at the expiry of a stated period, to whoever held the bill at that time and presented it for payment. The money was ultimately due by the borrower but, as King's signature appeared on the bills as well, anyone else who held the bill could obtain the money from him if the original borrower failed to meet his obligations. What King was lending, therefore, was his credit rather than any actual cash. He took on the responsibility that the noblemen might not meet their obligations. He was doubtless well paid for his complacence in taking this step, but he and Solomons made sure that they obtained more from the borrowers than this initial payment. Once the bills had been signed by both parties, they had to be turned into money by being discounted— sold at a discount from their face value to someone who would hold them until maturity or would sell them to someone else to hold to maturity. This was the process of the bill of exchange, which was used to a much greater extent in the early nineteenth century than it is today, for the financing of legitimate trade as well as shady transactions. In the ordinary processes of trade, a merchant who received a bill for £100 payable in three months' time would discount it with his bankers, receiving perhaps £98 at once instead of waiting three months to receive the full amount. The noblemen who borrowed on bills of exchange would expect to pay a higher rate of interest or, as it would be termed in this case, a greater rate of discount, and thus would expect to receive less than £98 for a £100 bill. One of the rivals of the King/ Solomons team, for example, a man named Wilson, in 1817 agreed to lend money to three impecunious and impatient young men. The three Marsacks brothers, all in their thirties, borrowed in anticipation of their inheritance from their wealthy father, who 'had attained the advanced age of 80 years, and could not be expected to survive much longer'. The bills were made payable six months after the death of Marsacks Senior, should one of his sons survive him—they were the special type of bill known as 'post-obits', by which heirs anticipated their future fortunes. The sons signed bills for a total of £15,000 in exchange for a promised immediate payment of £3,000—but in fact they were only able to screw £1,700 out of Wilson, having rashly handed the bills over before they had been paid. The father died two years later, but in 1827 the son who had inherited the estate was still engaged in lawsuits in his struggles to avoid redeeming in full the bonds he had signed ten years earlier.

The King/Solomons team, according to the story told later, would take as much advantage as it could of the difficulties of those who came to it for help. King would send his clients with the bill to Solomons to get it discounted; Solomons, under the name of Spencer, operated for this purpose from an office in Storey's Gate, in Westminster, a part of the world where noblemen would not be ashamed to be seen. However, they had not met all their obligations when they had paid King for his services and paid Ikey what was doubtless a high rate of discount: they were seldom given all the value of their bills in cash. They were given a little money, but would have to take most of it in the form of silver or other valuable articles, which they would then have to turn into money by pawning. This was a further loss for them and doubtless a gain for Ikey and, as they usually sent one of his servants out to pawn the goods, we can imagine that he would profit still further on the transaction. This, then, is the story which is told by the author of Ikey's biography.

There is no means of knowing whether what he says is true, about Ikey or about King. Young men of good family who got themselves into temporary financial difficulties were no doubt sometimes treated in the way described (the story of the borrowers being fobbed off with valuable goods rather than with cash is an old one—it appears in Molière's *L'Avare* of 1668.) But even if the general tale is true this may be just another case of evil-doings common in his day being laid at Ikey's door. Whatever the truth, the author ends his account of this part of Ikey's activities by saying that the game came to an end when one of Ikey's prostitutes found that a favoured customer had been taken in by the King/Solomons technique. She told the young man the whole story and revealed the connection between the banker and the discounter of the bills; in consequence, threats of prosecution were made to King and Solomons which forced them to abandon the house in Storey's Gate and their profitable association.

Then, says the author, Isaac Solomons took lodgings in Goodge Street and employed a number of young thieves. These he sent out to steal for him after the manner in which Fagin employed his little gang of boys. One of the exploits of these youngsters brought trouble to Ikey and to his confederate, John King. One of the boys had broken into a house in Percy Street belonging to a Colonel Napier, and the property stolen passed into the possession of Ikey Solomons. Some weeks later, the story runs, Ikey, when drinking in a coffee house, entered into conversation with another customer there and eventually sold to him a ring and a watch. The purchaser turned out to be Colonel Napier's steward and he recognized the ring and watch as having been stolen from Colonel Napier. The author of the account does not trouble to explain away the coincidence, or even to suggest why the steward should buy articles from a stranger in a coffee house—he is not said to have had any suspicion of Ikey to justify him in leading him on, and the whole transaction is highly improbable. Be that as it may, the story tells that a warrant was obtained for Ikey's arrest and an officer who was pursuing him followed him to John King's house. Although Ikey was hiding in the house, he was not found by the officer, but the search for him led to the connection between Solomons and King becoming known and this discredited King and led to a failure of his bank.

Following his policy of accusing Ikey of every imaginable crime, the author of 'The Life and Exploits' says that Ikey sold imitation cameo brooches as real ones and brass rings as gold, to drunken people in pubs. Ikey is said to have been put into Dover Gaol but to have bribed his way out and to have opened further brothels, one in Little May's Buildings and another in Mansell Street, Goodman's Fields. The latter brothel, it is said, was known as Solomons's synagogue, and was run by his wife. Ikey is accused of making a show of devoutness, and said to have been a regular attender to his religious duties. This was, however, only to evil ends: he used the locker which he, like other worshippers, was allocated in the synagogue to keep pornographic literature which one of his assistants was selling for him but which he did not want to keep at home or anywhere else, for 'he had the decency to keep them from the knowledge of his own family'. This implausible story betrays the author's desire to blacken Ikey at every turn. It is hardly likely that a man who employed his wife to direct his brothel would worry about her knowing that he sold pornographic literature, and the suggestion that he collected supplies of the literature each Sabbath, carrying it away in his pockets, is palpably absurd—it is a prohibition against carrying things on the Sabbath that leads to the provision of lockers in synagogues for worshippers' use, and detection would be even more certain than in the ordinary way.

Another version of Ikey's early life and later doings was published about the same time as 'The Life and Exploits' under the title 'Adventures, Memoirs, Former Trial, Transportation, and Escapes, of that Notorious Fence, and Receiver of Stolen Goods, Isaac Solomons; Better known to the Public by the Cognomen of Ikey Solomons; together with the Apprehension,

Trial, and Subsequent Transportation of Mrs. Solomons, and an
account of Her Husband's Ultimate Re-Apprehension in New
South Wales'. This writer says that Isaac on one occasion drove
to Windsor in a horse and chaise, 'enacting the gentleman'. He
picked up on the road a man who seemed to be a wealthy farmer,
who said he was on the way to Reading. Ikey explained that he
was spending the night at Windsor and urged his chance acquaintance to do the same; after a good dinner, he persuaded the
stranger to join him in a game of cards. The stranger, who had
been drinking pretty freely at Ikey's invitation, won at first but
then lost, and Ikey went to bed having won £35. The stranger
left the inn first in the morning and, when Ikey went to pay his
bill with one of the notes that he had won during the evening,
he found that they were forgeries. The stranger had taken good
money from Ikey when he was winning, and then had paid him
in worthless notes in the later stages of the evening, and had
gone off with £17.10.0 of Ikey's good money. The Great Ikey
had met a greater sharper than himself.

Like the writer of the 'Life and Exploits', the writer of this
second account alleges that Isaac Solomons had police officers in
his pay. He told how a clergyman 'who officiates not far from
the East India Docks' was knocked down and robbed in Caven-
dish Square. The clergyman lost money and valuables, including
a valuable silver snuff-box which found its way into Ikey's
hands. Suspicion somehow fell on Ikey and his associates, and
'to prevent anything being made public' he had to give back
all the property, with hush-money besides—'Ikey always took
care to reward these vigilant protectors of our property, by very
handsome donations, whenever a *delicate subject* of this nature was
in their hands'. There is no doubt, of course, that Ikey was a
highly successful receiver of stolen goods, nor is there any doubt
that at the time receivers of stolen goods often had police officers
in their pay and therefore this part of the tale may be more
accurate than some of the other stories told about Solomons. The
'Adventures, Memoirs' also accuses Ikey of a variety of crimes.
He is said to have become a leading figure in the trade of disposing
of goods smuggled into England. Gangs of his associates operated

in most towns in England, it is said; mainly foreigners, until a tightening of the residence rules for aliens made this difficult. About this time, too, the smuggling business became less satisfactory because of increased checks at the ports. Ikey began to combine smuggling with fraud: on one occasion he persuaded a London business house with a good reputation to buy some cambric still on board a French vessel in the River Thames, showing a sample of it. The sample was genuine cambric but the bulk of the goods was not, and Ikey obtained £194 for goods not worth £40—and the buyers, having attempted to buy goods which had not paid customs duty, could not complain.

There was a third pamphlet, 'The Life and Adventures of Isaac Solomons, The Notorious Receiver of Stolen Goods, Better Known as Ikey Solomons, from his Birth to the Present Time; with a Particular Account of his Extraordinary Escape from the City Officers; his Re-capture in New South Wales; and Trials at the Old Bailey, on Eight Different Indictments; To which are subjoined, The Life and Trial of Mrs. Solomons, the Wife of the Above'. However, its account of his early life is drawn from the 'Adventures, Memoirs' and it is only the reports of Ikey's trials that are new.

These, then, are some of the wild allegations which were made about Isaac Solomons and his early doings at the time of his downfall in 1829–30. All the stories cannot be true, but equally it is unlikely that they were all false. There is no evidence that Ikey was a brothel-keeper, or a money-lender. But he certainly was a receiver of stolen goods in a large way of business.

Many writers testify to the scale of Ikey's business by 1826. 'The Life and Exploits' describes him as probably one of the most successful fences in London. The author says that £18,000-worth of property was seized when Ikey was arrested. Charles Pelham, in his *Chronicles of Crime* of 1841, raises the figure to £20,000 and says that Ikey was the leading dealer in stolen bank-notes. A police magistrate told a select committee of the House of Commons in 1828 that Solomons kept a house 'where a considerable extent of business' was done. His house in Bell Lane, Spitalfields, someone wrote, was 'looked upon as the universal resort of almost all the thieves of the metropolis'. He was a well-known figure around Petticoat Lane, the great thieves' market, declared a constable of a Westminster parish, and was often in the Red Lion Inn in that street, which was 'frequented by Thieves and persons of bad character'. A newspaper in 1827 said of someone who was charged with receiving stolen goods 'the prisoner is said to have been for years, a second Ikey Solomons'. A writer in *Fraser's Magazine* in 1832 mentioned Ikey when claiming that 'the great and monied receivers are rarely or never brought to justice'. In 1838, when the writer of the playbill (the forerunner of our modern programme) for a performance of *Oliver Twist* at the Royal Surrey Theatre wanted to stress the authenticity of Dickens's picture of Fagin, it was to Solomons that he turned. 'The City officers,' he said, 'in pursuing that great receiver of stolen goods, Ikey Solomons, discovered cellars and trap doors, and all sorts of places of concealment, which they found full of stolen goods.' The novelist Arthur Morrison, writing in 1896 his book *A Child of the Jago*, was content to make a passing reference to 'the prince of fences, Ikey Solomons' without further explanation. Thus it is hardly surprising that when another and younger Isaac Solomons appeared at the Old Bailey in July, 1827, he told the Court 'I am no relation to *Ikey* Solomons and trust my name will not prejudice me'.

According to the author of 'The Life and Exploits', Solomons was 'allowed to be the most ready and superior judge of the intrinsic value of all kinds of property, from a glass bottle to a five hundred guinea chronometer; how it could be disposed of', and what its value was on the thieves' market. Pelham claimed that he established amongst thieves a regular rule of giving a fixed price for all articles of the same denomination. A piece of linen, says Pelham, was in his view a piece of linen, whether fine or coarse; the same with a piece of print, a silver watch, or a gold watch—'taking the good, as he used to tell the young and inexperienced thief, with the bad *vons*'. It was to this rule that Arthur Morrison referred in 1896, for the fictional fence of the Jago, like Ikey, followed this simple system. 'A breast pin brought a fixed sum, good or bad, and a velvet cloth brought the fixed

price of a roll of cloth, regardless of quality.' Pelham talks of
Ikey explaining the rule to young and inexperienced thieves and,
if there is any truth in the story at all, it was probably mainly
such people who let Ikey get away with it. Police officers of the
present day have known of fences using the system of a fixed
price for goods of a particular class, but the price set in these
cases is normally a very low one which is not acceptable to those
who are in a position to look around for a better one. If Ikey
did operate this system, it is likely that he was relying on the
custom of those who knew no other receivers or who needed
to dispose of their booty rapidly and had no time to shop around
for a better price.

According to Pelham, however, Ikey Solomons paid the
highest prices in London for stolen bank-notes. The gold
sovereign had re-entered active circulation in 1821, after the
financial upsets associated with the Napoleonic Wars. Notes for
£1 and £2 circulated as well, although they were to be withdrawn in 1829. However, in an age when banking and the use
of cheques was far less developed than at present, notes of higher
denominations were in relatively frequent use, despite the fact
that they had very much higher purchasing power than their
equivalents today. As the numbers of £5 notes or larger notes
were usually recorded, thieves could not readily cash them. Some
people were, however, prepared to accept stolen notes. A police
officer told a select committee of the House of Commons in 1817
that stolen bank-notes were sometimes found in the hands of
tradesmen who did not actually refuse to give any account of
how they came by them, but pretended not to know the names
of those who had given them the notes, even notes for £10,
£20 or £100. Clearly this could not often be done without
arousing suspicion, however, and it was found that the most
satisfactory method was to send the stolen notes to the Continent.
It was said that Ikey was able to outbid all rival receivers for
stolen bank-notes because of his connection with Jews in Holland.
The notes were allowed to circulate for a time on the Continent
but would eventually find their way to London firms who would
pay them into the Bank of England. The Continental firms might

E

well have been perfectly innocent, and would perhaps have received the notes at one of the large fairs on the Continent where business was frequently done for ready money and where debts were often paid in sterling. As the Bank of England could not contemplate the possibility that its notes would cease to be acceptable on the Continent, it had no alternative but to honour the bank-notes when they were presented. According to Pelham, Solomons paid 15 shillings in the £ for large bank-notes and, on average, it cost him 1 shilling in the £ to send them to the Continent and pass them through to the Bank. Ikey was thus earning a profit of 4 shillings in the £ on the nominal value of the notes which he handled. According to Pelham, his prices became the regular prices with all London fences. However, Ikey's rate for a £5 note was apparently only £3, and pick-pockets in the Westminster Bridewell in the 1830s claimed to get £4 or £4.10.0 for a fiver. Henry Mayhew, writing in 1851, gave the price of a £5 note on the illicit market as £3.10.0. It is, of course, very difficult to establish the facts about such a matter, but there seems no reason to doubt that Ikey Solomons was a leading fence in stolen bank-notes, even if his position was not quite as dominant as Pelham suggests.

Receivers did not always have to send bank-notes to the Continent to be disposed of. For notes of really large value and bonds and other valuable documents which were difficult to negotiate, they had another resource. The banks, to the regret of the authorities, were often ready to buy back their property for a proportion of its value, asking no questions and not seeking to establish who had committed the original theft. The select committee of the House of Commons which inquired into the state of the police of the metropolis in 1828 had no doubt about the matter. They said that they had 'directed their attention to these compromises for the restitution of stolen property, which general rumour and belief had represented so often to have taken place. They regret to say that their enquiries have proved such compromises to have been negotiated with an unchecked frequency and under an organized system far beyond what had been supposed to exist. . . . They have proof of more than sixteen banks having sought, by these means, to indemnify themselves for their losses; and that property of various sorts, to a value of about £200,000, has, within a few years, been the subject of negotiation or compromise.' All too often, it was one of the police officers who acted as go-between, getting in touch with a receiver of his acquaintance and arranging the exchange with him. This is what happened in one case in which we know that an Ikey Solomons (either our Ikey or another one) was involved, although, as it happens, it was not bank property but stolen jewellery which was being returned in this particular case.

Early in 1828, someone stole from Mr. Delafond, a jeweller of Sackville Street, near Regent Street, a handbook containing jewellery worth £800. Following the custom of the day, he applied to Bishop, one of the Bow Street officers, for assistance in obtaining the return of his property. Bishop recommended that Delafond should offer a reward of £100, but subsequently, doubtless because he had now found out how much was demanded by the criminals, told Delafond a different story. Bishop said that he now knew who had the stolen property, but he needed £350 in order to secure the return of the jewellery. Delafond offered £300, and in the end Bishop accepted this sum, which was paid to him. Bishop assured Delafond that a man would call on him that evening after seven p.m., bringing the box with the goods. About nine p.m. that evening a man did come, and he left the box with Mr. Delafond. The box was indeed the same one as that in which the goods had been sent out, but when the jeweller examined his property he found that about £50-worth of goods was missing. Delafond seems to have regarded this as an attempt to doublecross him and the consequence was that he wrote to the Home Secretary complaining about what had happened and demanding a full investigation. The Home Secretary promptly wrote to the magistrates of Bow Street, in his turn demanding from them a full examination of the facts.

Ten days later, the Home Secretary had received the report from the Bow Street magistrates. He summed up his view of the situation: 'It is clearly established that through the direct agency of Bishop, he being in communication with a man of

infamous character named Ikey Solomons, a party having lost
Property to a very considerable amount was able to recover
possession of that property on payment of three hundred pounds—
Payment was made personally by Bishop to Solomons thus
establishing a secret beneficial intercourse between one party
whose duty it was to detect Offenders and bring them to justice,
and another party directly concerned probably in those violations
of the Law which the Police ought to prevent or punish.' The
Home Secretary ordered that Bishop be dismissed. However, it
was just at this time that the select committee of the House of
Commons was receiving the evidence which enabled it to make
the trenchant declaration about the extent of compounding, and
in July, 1828, the Home Secretary wrote to the Bow Street
magistrates, saying that he had reconsidered the case. He allowed
Bishop to be reappointed to his position of police officer, as the
evidence which was given before the select committee on police
showed that his actions 'were in no way exceptional'.

All had thus ended happily for those concerned. Two points
remain to be made. First, it was only the attempt to cheat the
jeweller that brought the matter to the attention of the authorities:
if Delafond had been warned that £50-worth of jewellery was
missing, and had been able to take account of it in setting the
amount of the reward, no complaint would have been made to
the Home Office. It is noteworthy, however, that the value
of the missing jewellery was exactly the same as the reduction
that Delafond had insisted in making in the amount of the reward.
Perhaps if he had paid Bishop £350, he would have received
all his jewellery back. The second point demands that we anti-
cipate our story a little. As we shall see shortly, there is a gap in
the story of Ikey Solomons's life between 25th May, 1827, when
he escaped from custody on his way back to Newgate Prison,
and 10th July, 1828, when he sailed from Rio de Janeiro to
Australia. If we are correct in associating the Ikey Solomons who
negotiated with Bishop with our Ikey, then we have established
that, as late as March, 1828, Ikey was still in London and carrying
on his business. It is true that this would mean that Bishop was
negotiating with an escaped prisoner without seeking to arrest

him, which is perhaps unlikely. What is even more unlikely is that this aspect of the matter did not occur to the Home Office when recording their impressions of the case. The alternative, however, is that there were two Ikey Solomonses engaged in this business, which is admittedly not impossible, and that no one thought it necessary to indicate the distinction between the two Ikeys. We shall probably never know which explanation is the correct one. However, even if our Ikey was not involved in this case, there is little doubt that he at times was in contact with police officers as a normal part of the business of a receiver of that day.

One principal occupation of many receivers was the training of younger members of the criminal profession. The mind immediately turns to Fagin and the Artful Dodger in *Oliver Twist* when this topic is raised, and there is little doubt that the picture which Dickens presented was in essence true. There was, indeed, nothing particularly new about it—stories of pickpockets practising on accomplices or on coats to which a bell was fixed date back long before the nineteenth century. In Solomons's day and afterwards, similar stories were told, although there is no evidence to show that Ikey himself was engaged in training youngsters. Some receivers, however, had their gang of juveniles, kept under close control. For example, the select committee on police of 1828 was told by a court official that he had on one occasion, passing a vacant spot of ground, noticed a collection of boys, with a man in the midst of them doling out provisions from a basket he held in his hand. A police officer was standing talking to the man, and when the court official inquired what was happening, the officer explained to him: 'Here is an old thief, who keeps all these boys in pay, and comes out regularly in the middle of the day, and brings them their food, and receives the produce of their plunder'—yet the officer had no evidence, he said, on which he could arrest either man or boys. There are similar tales, making it clear that many receivers acted like Fagin, even if Ikey did not.

It was not only pickpockets who needed the services of youngsters. House-breakers found them useful, both as scouts and look-outs, and as a means of getting into premises. It will be remembered that Oliver Twist was used for this purpose by Bill Sikes, being put through a window into the house at Chertsey to open the doors for his masters. Forgers and coiners used youngsters as go-betweens, and a forged cheque would often be presented at a bank counter not by the true criminal but by some youngster who had been given sixpence or a shilling merely to cash it and to return the proceeds to a man waiting at the door. One twelve-year-old, who was employed by his father to pass false money, was asked what he was given for the work:'Plenty of victuals, and a penny-a-day if I did well' he replied, 'and a good hiding if I did not.' Moreover, youngsters would often be sent out by their parents to gain a specified sum in whatever way they could, by stealing, begging, sweeping a crossing, holding horses or anything else, on pain of a beating if they returned without it. The committee of 1828 was told 'It is no uncommon thing . . . to see infants of five, six, or seven years old, with a few matches in their hands, at ten, eleven, or twelve o'clock at night; and on being questioned why they do not go home, they answer that their mothers will beat them if they go without money, or at least that they shall get no supper.' As one such youngster said to the Chaplain of Newgate Prison, 'If I did not get anything I had no dinner or supper; and a handkerchief always fetches sixpence in Field Lane.'

Apart from the youngsters who were forced into crime by parents or other adults, there were those who had no other means of support. There was throughout the early part of the nineteenth century a large floating population of youngsters, living rough in the streets of London and the other large cities, with no home and no family. Dr. Barnado estimated as late as 1876 that there were about 30,000 neglected children under sixteen years old sleeping out on the streets of London, and this estimate may give us some indication of the number in Ikey's day. The youngsters would beg, pilfer or do anything else for which opportunity served, in order to raise a copper or two. One of them explained to Henry Mayhew, the great investigator of the 1850s, that the first twopence which was acquired in a day went to buy some food; the second twopence, if it came along, was used to buy a bed or the share of a bed in a common lodging house—and this was clearly a great boon on a cold winter's night; the third twopence, if fortune had been good, went on more food. Mayhew's informant apparently did not raise his sights beyond sixpence a day. Some youngsters could not afford entry to a lodging house and were refused admission to a refuge or a workhouse, places which would only receive them for a limited number of nights at a time. They would have to sleep out. They would sleep under the arches of bridges, in the barrows and carts around one of the city's markets before it opened, under house porches, or even under the trees of Hyde Park. Despite the frightful suffering which they must have endured, many of these youngsters continued to live by begging and petty crime, without seeking any alternative.

However, not all those who started life in this fashion were content to remain mere petty criminals. Those with more enterprise and intelligence would soon turn to the more profitable and more skilled branches of crime. (Dick, the Adelphi boy who was trained as a pickpocket, was one of this type, and Ikey was in the same class.) These youngsters selected themselves by intelligence, industry and drive. It was youngsters of this group who committed the more serious type of crime and thus received sentences of transportation to Australia, whereas those in the first group were usually merely imprisoned in this country for a month or three months. It is a melancholy fact that a youngster thrown on to the streets of London like Oliver Twist was really better off, materially at any rate, if he fell into the hands of a Fagin than if he was left to his own devices. (There were in real life a few kindly people like Mr. Brownlow, but far too few to meet the need.) And if one thinks of oneself in such a circumstance, then one can only hope to have had the enterprise and ability to be an Artful Dodger rather than a Noah Claypole, one can only hope that one would have become a skilled criminal and rapidly earned transportation to Australia. The Artful Dodger's friends were, after all, prepared to think well of him because he was being transported to Australia very early in life.

' "Never mind, Charlie," said Fagin soothingly . . . "Think how young he is too! What a distinction, Charlie, to be lagged at his time of life!" "Well, it is an honour, that is," said Charlie, a little consoled.' Sad though it is, one can see what they mean.

Chapter Four

ESCAPE, CAPTURE, ESCAPE

The first check to Ikey's long and successful career as one of London's leading fences came in May, 1826. He had to make himself scarce because someone appeared at his house with a search warrant for stolen property—property which was in fact concealed there. A few months previously, on the night of the 22nd/23rd December, 1825, a warehouse in George Yard, Lombard Street, in the City of London, had been broken into. It belonged to Messrs. McCabe and Strachan, watchmakers in Cornhill in the City, and about £200-worth of property, mainly watch movements, had been stolen. In Ikey's day a serious investigation for stolen property was only carried out in cases where the victim of the crime spent time and money on a pursuit of the offenders—and unfortunately for Ikey, this was one of those cases. Charles Strachan, one of the partners, devoted considerable attention to the task of finding his stolen watch movements. In May, 1826, Strachan received information—the nature of which, in the best tradition, he did not disclose in court—as a consequence of which he obtained a warrant for the search of Ikey's house in Bell Lane, near Petticoat Lane, Spitalfields. Strachan, with James Stafford, one of his men, and two police officers, Foster and Fortune, arrived at the house between ten and eleven on a Sunday morning. Ann Solomons told him that her husband was out but that she was expecting him back for breakfast at any moment; she showed them into the parlour where the table was laid for breakfast and asked them to wait. After about a quarter of an hour, however, Strachan became restive and the party began to search the house without waiting for Solomons. At the top of the house there was a room with a padlocked door.

As they were examining this door, Ikey arrived. He naturally inquired what the visitors wanted. When he was told Strachan's name and why he was there, he felt his pockets, and then said he would go down and get the key—and promptly disappeared and was not seen again. About ten minutes later, Ikey's father appeared and told Strachan and the officers that Ikey was still hunting for the key. The party agreed to wait until twelve noon. However, while they were waiting, they heard noises from inside the padlocked room as if someone were trying to break into it from outside and they therefore broke the door down and entered it themselves. 'We were covered with a cloud of lime dust'—someone had been trying to break into the locked room through the ceiling. Sure enough, five of the stolen watch movements were found in the room. Ikey had evaded the searchers, but now there was evidence against him on a charge of receiving stolen property and a warrant for his arrest was issued.

Ikey managed to get safely away from his pursuers. We do not know where he lived or spent his time for most of the period after his escape, but he was clearly able to carry on his business, for most of the charges on which he was eventually tried related to property which was not stolen until after May, 1826. We know, however, that in March, 1827, he went to lodge with a Mrs. Jane Oades in Lower Queen Street, Islington, near its junction with George Street. He took one room on the first floor and lived there under the name of Jones, sleeping and eating in the same room, until he was arrested a month later. At his trial, Mrs. Oades testified that 'During the time the prisoner continued at my lodgings he always behaved like a gentleman'. His wife, Mrs. Oades said, visited him at Lower Queen Street but did not stay there. It seems that Ikey was lying low and giving his wife instructions regarding the carrying on of his business while the police officers, at the instigation of Charles Strachan, hunted for him.

It was not until April, 1827, that Ikey's luck ran out. On Monday, the 23rd of that month, he was recognized in the New North Road, Islington, by James Lea, a police officer of the Lambeth Street Office, who promptly arrested him. Lea may just have been lucky enough to run into Isaac in the street, but there may have been more to it than that. Charles Strachan had had a 'long interview', it is recorded, with John Hardwick, one of the magistrates of the Lambeth Street Office, and Lea was 'acting under his directions'. Perhaps the experienced magistrate and the experienced police officer had between them more than just luck to rely upon. Indeed, they may have had help from someone close to Ikey. One of the accounts of Ikey's life says that he was betrayed to Lea by a slighted mistress. He is supposed to have had a long association with this woman but to have broken it off. Taking advantage of his enforced absence from home after Strachan's call at his house, the story goes, he had ceased to meet her. However, she found out where he was staying and wanted to renew the friendship—and when Ikey 'repulsed her advances . . . she, in revenge, gave information to the police, of his residence and the places in which his stolen property was concealed'. Another account has a slightly different version. His wife, it says, discovered the existence of the other woman and her threats of vengeance made Ikey decide to leave the country; it was the effort to realize all his assets that attracted the attention of the police. The two stories, despite their differences, suggest a belief at the time that the cause of Ikey's arrest lay in his love affairs; and this cautionary tale may be true.

When Lea arrested Ikey he took his prisoner to Islington watch-house and searched him. Ikey was found to have on him a great quantity of watches, jewellery and cash: '180 sovereigns, three £10 and three £5 notes of the Bank of England, a gold watch . . . a silver engine-turned watch . . . a fine gold watch-chain with barrelled slips, a link gold chain with three small seals, topaz, white cornelian and amythest, an old-fashioned seal resembling a masonic arch with a bust of Wellington, a plain seal with the initials IS surmounted by masonic emblems with an anchor underneath, a diamond pin of the table form and a masonic seal, topaz.' Ikey was lodged in the Whitechapel watch-house overnight, being detained on the McCabe and Strachan charge. Other accusations were soon brought against him; they resulted from a routine police measure, the search of the residence of an arrested man. (It is usually accepted that no warrant is needed for such a search, although there is no statute or recognized rule of common law conferring the right.)

The morning after Ikey's arrest, at about six a.m., James Lea went to Mrs. Oades's house. He was only just in time—Ann Solomons and one of her sons were outside the house, in a coach, and doubtless would soon have removed any incriminating evidence if they had had the chance. But Lea would not let them go into the house. He knocked and asked Mrs. Oades if she had a lodger named Solomons. She replied that she had not, but that a man called Jones occupied a room on the first floor. Lea, with Robert Davies, one of his fellow-officers, went up to 'Jones's' room, and there, Lea said later, they found 'a vast quantity of property, lace, handkerchiefs, veils, Irish linen, table-cloths, and various articles, silk handkerchiefs, a watch, some bobbinet, and a quantity of caps; all the property was tied up in bundles, under the bedstead—there were three or four large bundles, and a great quantity of valencia waistcoat pieces; I took it all away—there was a large trunkful; all the articles were new, and might be worth £300 or £400 altogether'. Davies added that there was a coachful of property, 'more than a man could carry'.

On Wednesday, 25th April, Ikey appeared in court before Matthew Wyatt and John Hardwick, two of the stipendiary magistrates of the Lambeth Street Police Office. He was charged as 'Isaac Solomons alias Ikey Solomons alias Jones'. This was the usual appearance of a prisoner before magistrates as soon as possible after his arrest, so that the justification for his continued detention can be established. Often all that happens when the prisoner first appears in court is that the police give evidence that they arrested the prisoner at a particular place and date on a particular charge, this formal step being followed by a remand to allow time for the case to be prepared. It was, however, possible to go beyond evidence of arrest in Ikey's case, even so soon after he had been captured. Strachan appeared in court to give evidence of finding his property in Solomons's house, after one of the McCabe and Strachan employees had given the necessary testimony to the facts of the warehouse-breaking. James Isaacs, appearing for Ikey, then applied to the magistrates for a week's remand, which was granted. Isaacs was however unsuccessful in another application, for the return of all the property found in Ikey's possession apart from that which was the subject of the McCabe and Strachan charge. The magistrates refused this request and ordered the usual invitation to be issued to people who hoped to identify property which had been stolen from them.

Much of the property found at Lower Queen Street was identified as stolen. One of the charges subsequently brought against Ikey, for example, concerned the following hotch-potch of goods found in Mrs. Oades's house: seventy-seven pieces of lace, containing 1,770 yards, value £40; forty-three handkerchiefs, value £5; twenty-eight veils, value £15; forty-three caps, with lappets, value £7.10.0; 357 other caps, value £19; thirty collars, value 15 shillings; 468 cap crowns, value £4; and forty pieces of bobbinet, containing 120 yards, value £8. Many of the charges on which Ikey was ultimately tried concerned property which was found in his room in Islington on this occasion.

Ikey appeared again before the magistrates on Tuesday, 1st May. He was far from well—'such an effect the little confinement he had sustained produced on a generally sickly frame, that the worthy magistrates acceded to the request of Ikey, and allowed him a chair'. Ikey is said to have offered McCabe and Strachan £200 to drop the charge against him, and to have promised a Lambeth Street officer £1,000 if he was allowed to escape. It would certainly have been worth his while to pay sums as large as these to avoid being arrested, for now other charges began to be made against him as people identified their property among the pile of goods found in Islington.

Not all the cases which were commenced against Ikey could be sustained in court. For example, he was charged with having possession of property worth £450 belonging to Hercule Paynter, but as Paynter's servant was not completely certain in his identification of the goods the magistrates dismissed the charge. However, sufficient evidence against Ikey was brought forward to make Mr. Adolphus, his counsel, realize that he could not prevent his being committed for trial on some charges, and he left the court, entrusting what little could be done to Isaacs. James Isaacs, of Bury Street, St. Mary Axe, in the City of London, was acting for Solomons in the way that a solicitor would today, although he does not seem to have been legally qualified and is described merely as Ikey's 'agent'. It was not until 1843 that the Solicitors' Act prevented unqualified persons from acting in that capacity.

The hearing of the charges against Ikey was not completed on 1st May, and he appeared again at the police office on Tuesday, 15th May. On that day he was committed to stand his trial at the Old Bailey on six charges, including the McCabe and Strachan case. In consequence of this committal, Ikey was transferred to Newgate Prison, making the second of his three known visits there.

Newgate was the oldest of the London prisons. Although the date of its origin is not known, it was certainly in existence by 1190. It remained a principal place of confinement until 1881, and continued to house prisoners awaiting execution or trial at the nearby Old Bailey until its demolition in 1902–3. In the early days and for much of its long life, it was notorious for over-crowding, lack of air and water, and epidemics. Attempts at improving the building were made from time to time. In 1241 a group of wealthy Jews of London was made to pay 20,000 marks (the mark was an old unit of currency equal to two-thirds of a pound) for the purpose—on penalty of being confined in the prison themselves. Part of Richard Whittington's property was, after his death, used to rebuild the gaol, and this building, erected in about 1425, lasted until the latter part of the eighteenth century, despite damage in the Great Fire of 1666. By that time conditions in the medieval prison were very bad, and John Howard, the great prison reformer, was very critical of Newgate. In 1777 he wrote that 'The prisoners were kept in close rooms, cells, and clammy dungeons fourteen or fifteen hours out of the twenty-four. The floors of some of those cabins were very damp—in some of them there was an inch or two of water, and straw and miserable bedding was laid upon the floors.' Rebuilding had in fact already begun—it started in 1767, and was completed in 1783, after repair of the damage caused in 1780 during the Gordon Riots, when the prison was set on fire. However, Howard was not greatly impressed with the results of the rebuilding.

In the early nineteenth century official visitors to Newgate continued to be critical. In 1808, two years before Ikey's first visit to the gaol, Sir Richard Philips, one of the sheriffs of the City of London and thus one of the prison's rulers, was critical of the crowding and the lack of air. He said that he had been 'shocked to see boys of thirteen, fourteen, and fifteen confined for months in the same yard with hardened, incorrigible offenders. Among the women, all the ordinary feelings of the sex are outraged by their indiscriminate association. The shameless victims of lust and profligacy are placed in the same chamber with others who, however they may have offended the laws in particular points, still preserve their respect for decency and decorum. . . . When the female prisoners lie down on their floors at night, there must necessarily, at least in the women's wards, be the same bodily contact and the same arrangement of heads and legs as in the deck of a slave-ship. The wards being only forty-three feet wide, admit by night of two rows to lie down at once in a length of thirty-seven feet; that is to say, twenty-five or thirty women, as it may be, in a row, having each a breadth of eighteen inches by her length.'

In 1818, between Ikey's first two visits, the Honourable Henry Gray Bennet, M.P., Chairman of a select committee of the House of Commons on the police and crime of the metropolis, was also sharply critical of the organization of Newgate Prison. At that time, although the prison was supposed to hold only 427 prisoners, the numbers were often 800, and occasionally even as many as 1,200. Bennet spoke harshly of the way in which the Grand Jury of Middlesex, whose duty it was to examine the prison and report on any defects, had performed its task. 'They could not have noticed the want of proper classification, nor the state of the condemned cells, nor the manner in which the prisoners sleep, nor the promiscuous assemblages of all kinds of misdemeanants in the five yards, nor the want of separation of old and young offenders in all parts of the prison.' The Grand Jury had referred to a 'slight want of matting and covering' but, said Bennet, it is 'in fact a want of proper rugs and bedding'. He was critical, too, of 'the nudity or the deficiency of shirts, shoes, and stockings'. In fact, the prisoners were not provided with clothing, nor with bedding. As a turnkey told Elizabeth Fry when she commenced her work about the time of Bennet's visit, 'You see, lady, straw ain't "allowed" here free, nor in most prisons it ain't. Prisoners gets it as pays for it. If we gave it we'd have to pay for it ourselves, and it would soon mount up, ye see.' A later official answer to a similar complaint was to point out that if every prisoner was given a bed there would not be enough floor-space to accommodate them! In this respect, as in others, charity went some way to fill the gap left by the official rules. The sheriffs ran a fund to which visitors contributed and from which some clothing and bedding was provided for the needy.

Bennet recorded that in the prison 'there was no separation of the young from the old, the children of either sex from the most ardent criminal. Boys of the tenderest years, and girls of the ages of ten, twelve and thirteen were exposed to the vicious contagion that predominated in all parts of the prison; and drunkenness prevailed to such an extent, and was so common, that unaccompanied with riot it attracted no notice.' Prostitutes were allowed to visit the prisoners on the pretext that they were their wives, and on payment of a fee of a shilling were allowed to remain in the wards during the night. A new keeper had been appointed just about this time and was beginning an attempt at reform, and undoubtedly conditions were better by Ikey's second stay in 1827. One change of which he will have been glad was that prisoners were no longer made to wear leg-irons. At the time of Ikey's first stay in Newgate even those awaiting trial were thus treated, mainly as a badge to distinguish prisoners from visitors. In 1818 improved arrangements for the control of visitors had made this no longer necessary.

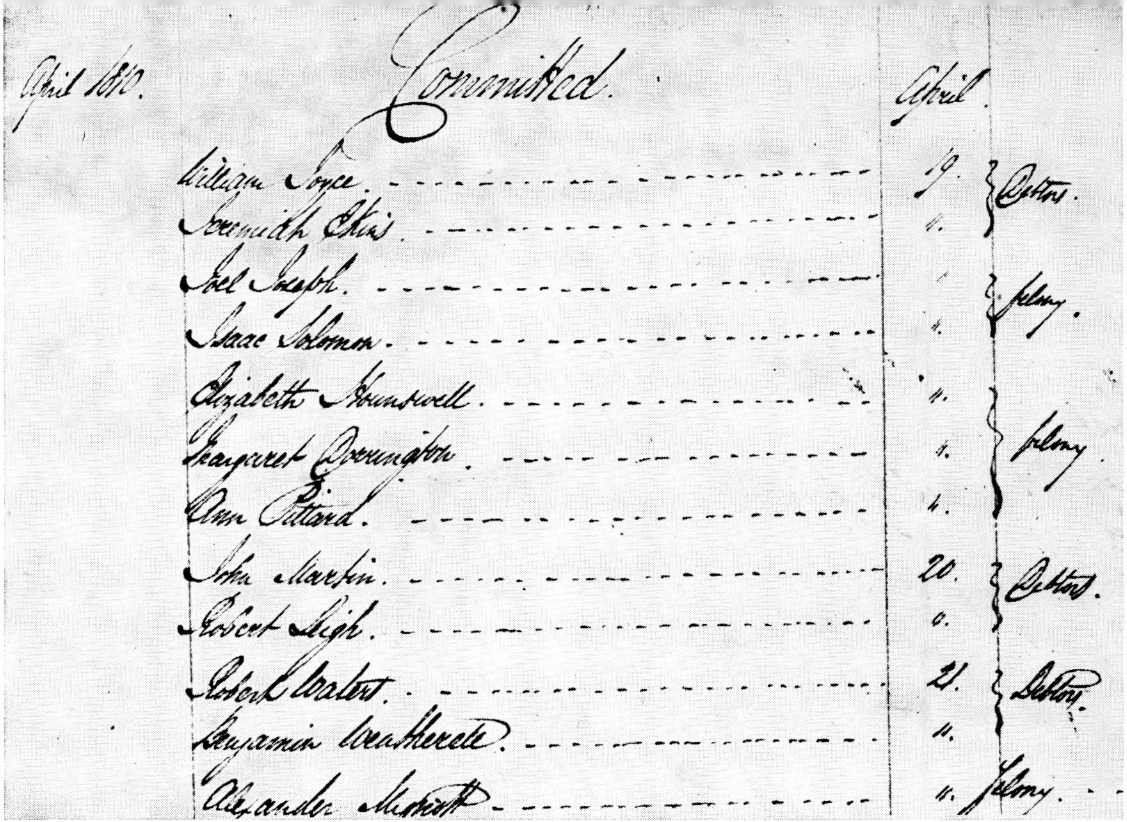
April 1810. Committed.

		April	
	William Joyce	19.	Debtors.
	Jeremiah Atkins	"	
	Joel Joseph	"	Felony.
	Isaac Solomon	"	
	Elizabeth Hounsewell	"	
	Margaret Covington	"	Felony.
	Ann Pittard	"	
	John Martin	20.	Debtors.
	Robert Leigh	"	
	Robert Walters	21.	Debtors.
	Benjamin Weathercote	"	
	Alexander Moffatt	"	Felony.

PLATE I Isaac Solomons's First Entry into Newgate in April 1810—The register of Newgate Gaol

(Pri Com 2/185, Public Records Office)

Name, Age, and Description	When brought into Custody.	By whom Committed	Offence charged with	When Tried, and Before whom.	Verdict.	Sentence.	How Disposed of.
[illegible]	*1827*	*[illegible]*	*[illegible]*				*[illegible]*
Detained			*[illegible]*				
Detained			*[illegible]*				
Detained			*[illegible]*				
Detained			*[illegible]*				
William Carter *[illegible]*	16 *[illegible]*	*[illegible]*	*[illegible]*	*[illegible]*			*[illegible]*
[illegible] Solomon [illegible]		*[illegible]*		*[illegible]*			Do

PLATE 2   The Record of Ikey's Arrest in 1827—The register of Newgate Gaol

(Pri Com 2/199, Public Records Office)

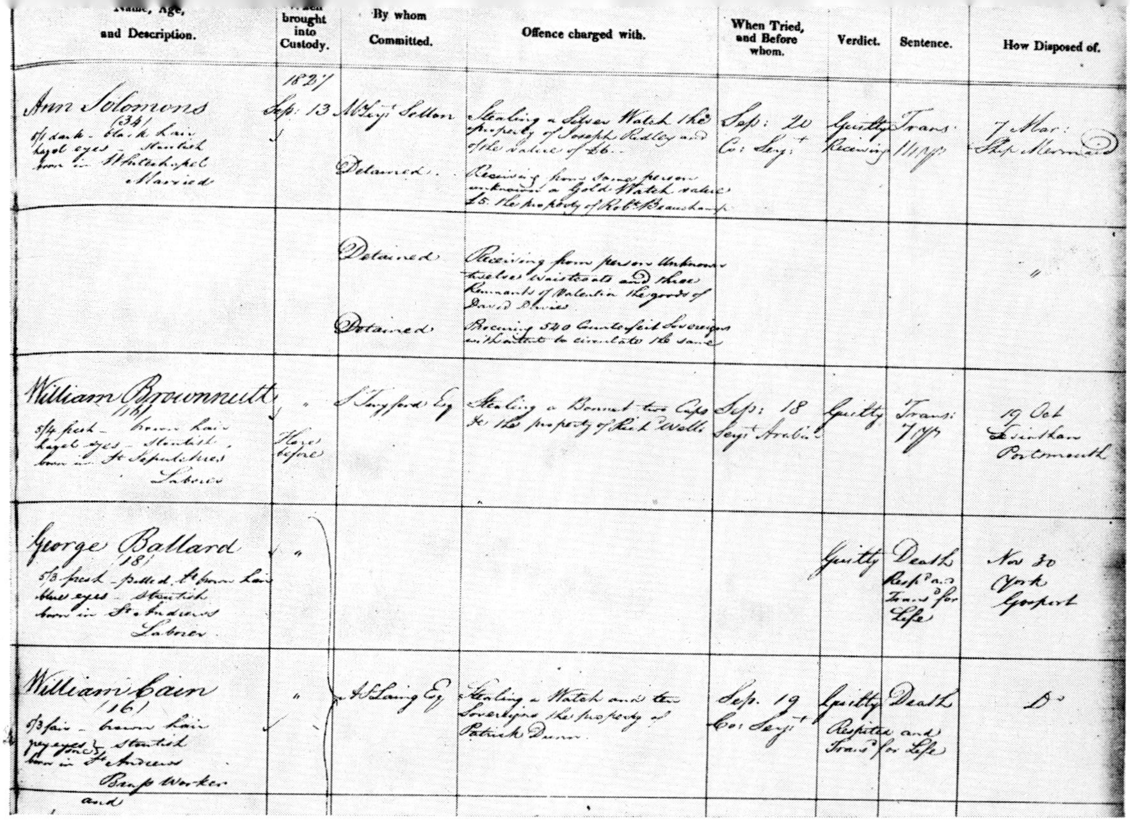

Name, Age, and Description.	When brought into Custody.	By whom Committed.	Offence charged with.	When Tried, and Before whom.	Verdict.	Sentence.	How Disposed of.
Ann Solomons (34) 5f dark - black hair hazel eyes - Stoutish born in Whitechapel Married	1827 Sep: 13	Mr Serjt Sellon	Stealing a Silver Watch the property of Joseph Ridley and of the value of £6	Sep: 20 Co: Serjt	Guilty Receiving	Trans: 14 yrs	7 Mar: Ship Mermaid
		Detained	Receiving from some person unknown a Gold Watch value £5 the property of Robt Beauchamp				
		Detained	Receiving from person unknown twelve Waistcoats and three Remnants of Valentia the goods of David Davies				"
		Detained	Receiving 540 Counterfeit Sovereigns with intent to circulate the same				
William Brownnutt (16) 5/4 fresh - brown hair hazel eyes - Stoutish born in St Sepulchres Labourer	" Here before	S Twyford Esq	Stealing a Bonnet two Caps &c the property of Richd Wallis	Sep: 18 Serjt Arabin	Guilty	Trans: 7 yrs	19 Oct Leviathan Portsmouth
George Ballard (18) 5/3 fresh - pitted, lt brown hair blue eyes - Stoutish born in St Andrews Labourer	"				Guilty	Death Respd and Transd for Life	Nov 30 York Gosport
William Cain (16) 5/3 fair - brown hair grey eyes - Stoutish born in St Andrews Brass Worker and	"	A Laing Esq	Stealing a Watch and ten Sovereigns the property of Patrick Dunn	Sep. 19 Co: Serjt	Guilty	Death Respited and Transd for Life	Do

PLATE 3 Ann follows Ikey into Newgate—The register of Newgate Gaol

(Pri Com 2/199, Public Records Office)

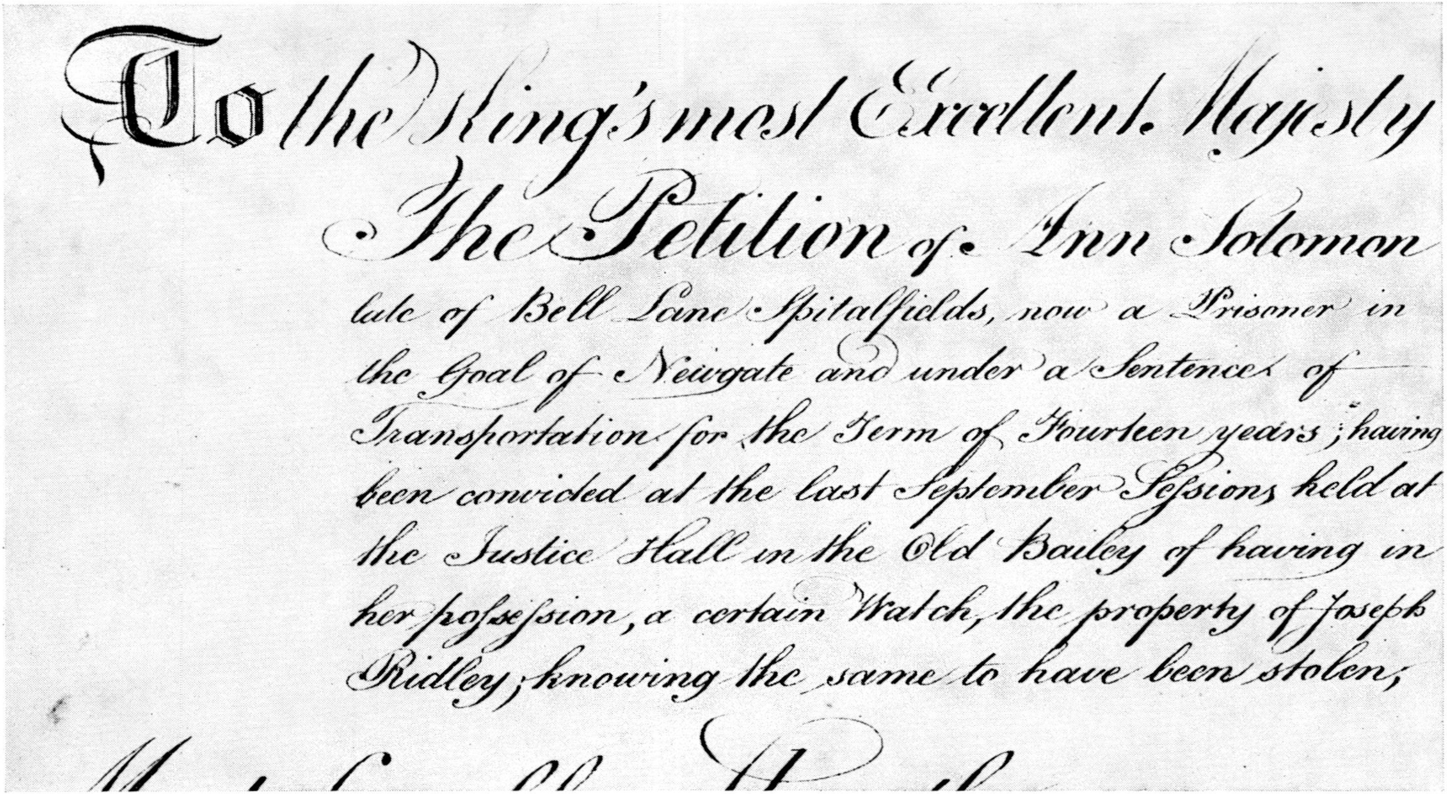

To the King's most Excellent Majesty
The Petition of Ann Solomon
late of Bell Lane Spitalfields, now a Prisoner in
the Goal of Newgate and under a Sentence of
Transportation for the Term of Fourteen years; having
been convicted at the last September Sessions held at
the Justice Hall in the Old Bailey of having in
her possession, a certain Watch, the property of Joseph
Ridley, knowing the same to have been stolen;

PLATE 4 The Opening Words of Ann Solomons's Petition—see Appendix IIIa

(*H.O. 17/107, Public Records Office*)

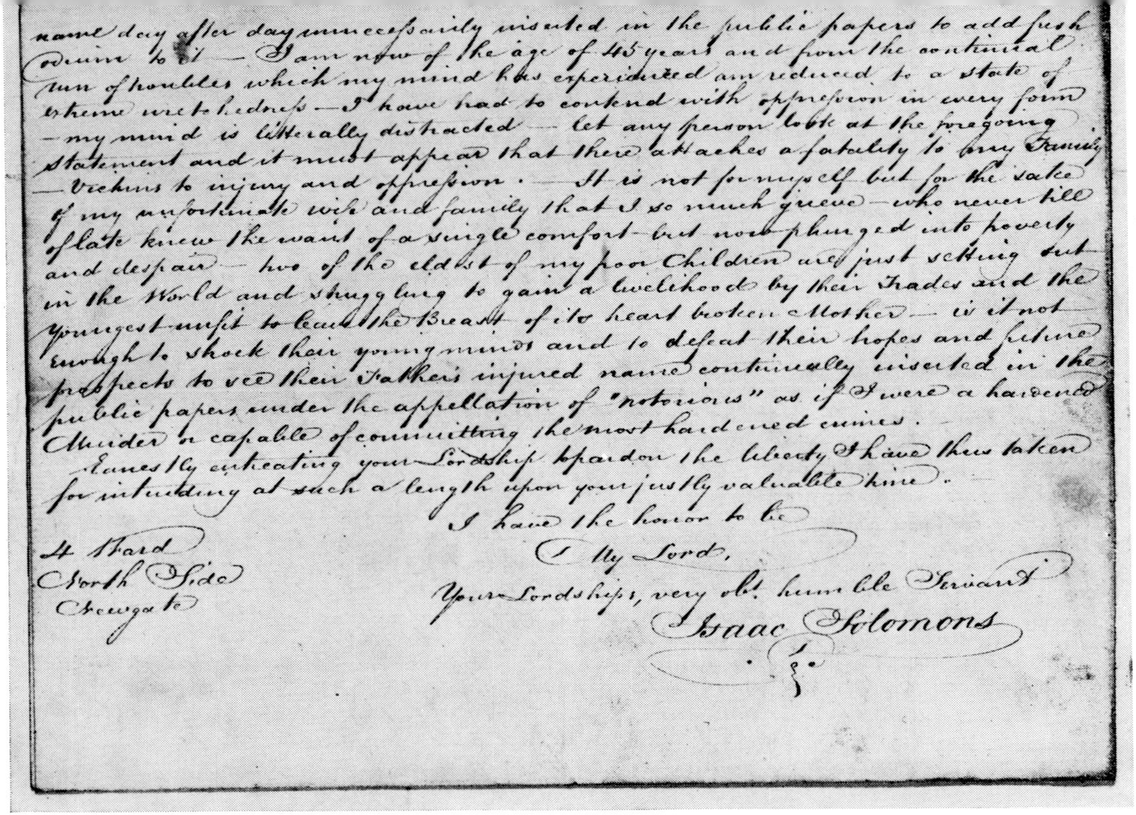

name day after day unnecessarily inserted in the public papers to add fresh
odium to it — I am now of the age of 45 years and from the continual
run of troubles which my mind has experienced am reduced to a state of
extreme wretchedness — I have had to contend with oppression in every form
— my mind is litterally distracted — let any person look at the foregoing
Statement and it must appear that there attaches a fatality to my Family
— victims to injury and oppression. — It is not for myself but for the sake
of my unfortunate wife and family that I so much grieve — who never till
of late knew the want of a single comfort — but now plunged into poverty
and despair — two of the eldest of my poor Children are just setting out
in the World and struggling to gain a livelihood by their Trades and the
youngest unfit to leave the Breast of its heart broken Mother — is it not
enough to shock their young minds and to defeat their hopes and future
prospects to see their Father's injured name continually inserted in the
public papers under the appellation of "notorious" as if I were a hardened
Murderer or capable of committing the most hardened crimes. —

Earnestly entreating your Lordship to pardon the liberty I have thus taken
for intruding at such a length upon your justly valuable time.

I have the honor to be
My Lord,
Your Lordships, very obt. humble Servant
Isaac Solomons

4 Ward
North Side
Newgate

PLATE 5 The Closing Words of Ikey's Petition—see Appendix V

PLATE 6   Ann Solomon's Convict Records—see Appendix I

(from original in the Archives Office of Tasmania)

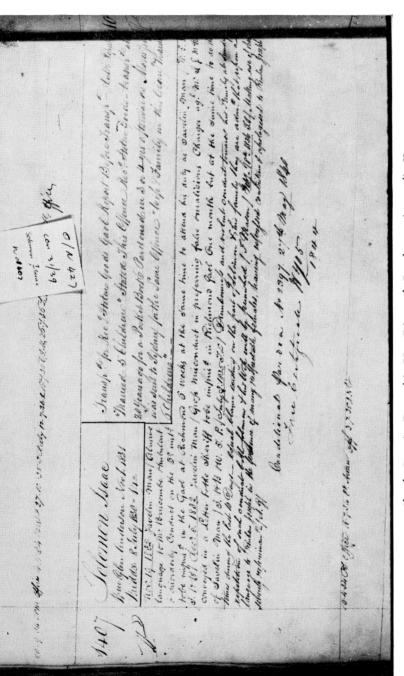

PLATE 7 Ikey's Convict Record in Van Diemen's Land—see Appendix II

(from original in the Archives Office of Tasmania)

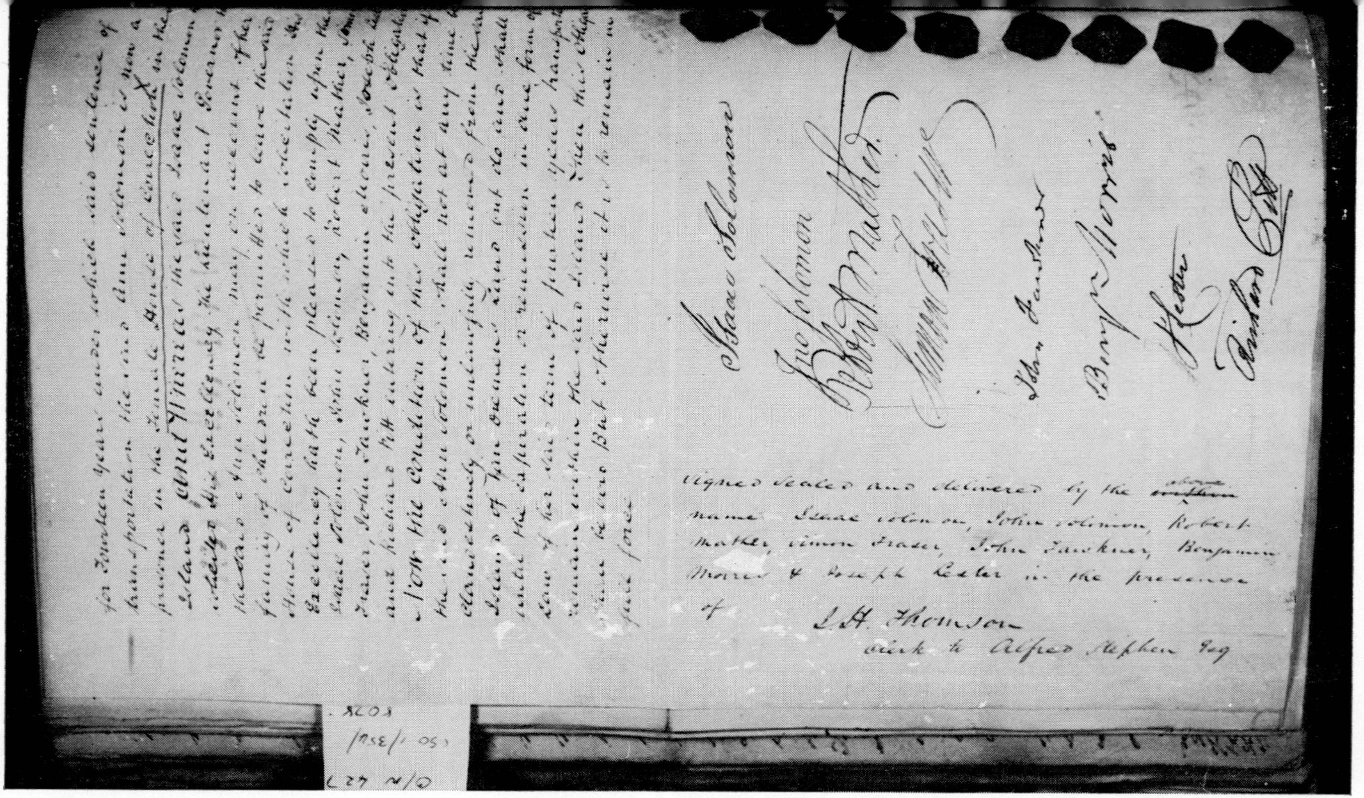

for Fourteen years under which said sentence of transportation the said Ann Solomon is now a prisoner in the Female House of Correction in the Island And Whereas the said Isaac Solomon solicited His Excellency the Lieutenant Governor that the said Ann Solomon may on account of her family of children be permitted to leave the said House of Correction with which solicitation His Excellency hath been pleased to comply upon the Isaac Solomon, John Solomon, Robert Mather, Simon Fraser, John Fawkner, Benjamin Morris, Joseph Lester and Richard Pitt entering into the present Obligation Now the Condition of this obligation is that if the said Ann Solomon shall not at any time be clandestinely or unlawfully removed from the said Island of Van Diemens Land but do and shall until the expiration or remission in due form of Law of her said term of fourteen years transportation remain within the said Island Then this Obligation shall be void But otherwise it is to remain in full force

Isaac Solomon
Jno Solomon
Robert Mather
Simon Fraser
John Fawkner
Benjn Morris
J Lester
Richard Pitt

Signed sealed and delivered by the above named Isaac Solomon, John Solomon, Robert Mather, Simon Fraser, John Fawkner, Benjamin Morris & Joseph Lester in the presence of
J.H. Thomson
Clerk to Alfred Stephen Esq

8203
(50/1350)
C/N 427

PLATE 8 Signature of Isaac Solomons and Others to Bond—see Appendix IV

(from original in the Archives Office of Tasmania)

By the time the Solomons family visited Newgate in force, in the 1820s, the state of hygiene of the prison had much improved. The surgeon, W. H. Cox, his son, N. J. Cox, or his assistant, Joe Seevar, visited the prison daily, recording their observations in a book kept for the inspection of the sheriffs and aldermen of the City. The following comment is typical: 'Friday 25th May, 1827. Visited every part of the prison. It is clean and in good order. Cases of ague and fever occur daily but no cases of any infectious nature have occurred. The patients [in the hospital] are all improving in health.' On most days the report is more laconic, although sometimes details of the cases in the hospital are recorded. There was an outbreak of 'inflammatory fever'—probably influenza—in February 1828, by which time Isaac, Ann and Henry Solomons had all passed through the prison. The surgeon ascribed the outbreak, which he first noted on 26th February, to 'the continuous damp weather'; three days later he noted that there were no fresh cases, but on 5th March he wrote 'inflammatory fever has been prevalent'. On the whole, however, reading the surgeon's report for a period of years gives the impression that the general level of health of the prisoners was good, even allowing for a certain official complacency.

However, the general atmosphere of the prison was unchanged for many years. The Inspectors of Prisons appointed in 1835, after Ikey Solomons had paid his third and final visit to Newgate, reported: 'The days were passed in idleness, debauchery, riotous quarrelling, immoral conversation, gambling, instruction in all nefarious processes, lively discourse on past criminal exploits, elaborate discussion of others to be perpetrated after release. No provision whatever was made for the employment of prisoners. . . . Drink, in more or less unlimited quantities, was still to be had. . . . Women saw men if they merely pretended to be wives; even boys were visited by their sweethearts.' Edward Gibbon Wakefield, having spent some time in Newgate, declared in 1831 his view that it was 'a great nursery of crime'.

Prisoners in Newgate were required to pay a multitude of fees to the gaolers. Every felon entering the master's side, where conditions were rather better than elsewhere, had to pay ten

F

shillings and sixpence, and the Press Yard, the most desirable part of the prison, demanded a three guinea admission fee. Fees were payable on discharge as well. Every felon discharged had to pay eighteen shillings and ten pence, and every prisoner charged with the less serious offences classed as misdemeanours had to pay fourteen shillings and tenpence. Three shillings and tenpence was payable to the gaoler by those who left Newgate on being pardoned, twenty-five shillings by petty offenders, who might perhaps have only been fined one shilling, and eight shillings and tenpence by debtors. In addition, the clerk was entitled to six shillings and twopence for every felon discharged, ten shillings for every misdemeanant, and four shillings and tenpence from every person convicted of petty larceny. All these fees to the keeper and his warders had to be paid before a prisoner could be discharged, and someone who had completed his sentence or had paid his fine but not met his fees would be retained in gaol. So too would someone who was acquitted, unless he had paid the required amount. Parliament made repeated attempts to change this practice but did not succeed until it introduced the rule—still existing at the present day—that immediately on acquittal the prisoner, in person or through his counsel, applies to the magistrate or the judge for his discharge and is immediately freed: he walks out of the court without returning to the prison.

In addition to these fees on entering and leaving the prison, felons had to contribute towards the cost of coal and candles, etc. On the master's side about thriteen shillings a week was paid, and on the common side about eight shillings a week. Anyone who was too poor even to pay the eight shillings on the common side had to do extra work in washing and cleaning the wards of the prison. On the master's side beds and bedding were furnished by the gaoler at the cost of two shillings and sixpence a week; the women felons were furnished with 'barrack bedsteads laid on the floor'. A woman named Ann Sell, a member of the company of free Vintners who had the right to sell wine in the City, had a room in the prison where she supplied prisoners with wine, and she also sold beer obtained from a nearby public house, charging twopence a gallon extra for the privilege.

The prisoners in Newgate, especially in the earlier part of the nineteenth century, had as much to fear from their fellows as from anyone else. The vicious system known as 'garnish' or 'chummage' demanded that each new arrival should buy drinks for all other inhabitants of the ward into which he was put. If he had not enough money to pay, his clothes would be taken and sold for the purpose. Thomas Fowell Buxton, an advocate of prison reform, described the case of a young lawyer who was brought before a court of prisoners because he refused to join in the drinking which took place after he had unwillingly paid his chummage. As he could not provide further money to be freed of the badgering of the other prisoners, he was frequently tried and punished by this court for a whole variety of offences such as 'coughing maliciously to the disturbance of his companions'. Eventually, he gave in and agreed to drink with them and then 'by insensible degrees he began to lose his repugnance to their society, caught their flash terms and sang their songs, was admitted to their revels and acquired, in place of habits of perfect sobriety, a taste for spirits'.

Much of the work of the prison, including the important task of serving out the food, was carried out by wardsmen who were themselves prisoners. The wardsmen bought their place from the turnkeys, and Bennet reported that one prisoner had offered fifty guineas for the place of wardsman but had been refused, because a higher price had been paid by someone else. Clearly the wardsmen were able to recoup these sums of money from their fellow prisoners.

A macabre feature of Newgate Prison in Ikey Solomons's day was the condemned sermon—the sermon preached at a service in the chapel which those who were about to be executed were required to attend. In the centre of the chapel was the condemned pew, an oval-shaped black box, large enough to hold thirty prisoners. A coffin was placed on a table in the middle of the pew. The other prisoners crowded into the chapel to stare at the men who were to die and, until 1826, the general public were admitted to the galleries on payment of a shilling. When the public ceased to be admitted, the women prisoners were given a place in one of the galleries, screened by curtains. As a final macabre touch, those who had been reprieved were given places in the front row of the gallery, so that they could get a good view of their former associates.

The prisoners who were to be executed made their last appearance in the chapel from the condemned cells, a part of the prison which had survived from the earlier building. These cells were nine feet long and six feet wide, with a vaulted roof and a small grated window. The walls were lined with planks, which were studded with nails. There were often about twenty prisoners there, mostly those waiting to hear if the sentence of death passed upon them was actually to be carried out or not. They usually had to wait about six weeks to learn their fate. The decision was taken by the Privy Council, and the warders were very critical of what happened: 'Those whom we know to be most guilty often escape, whilst those whom we know to be least guilty often suffer—it is all a lottery.' The news whether they were to be executed or respited was brought to the men under sentence of death by the Ordinary of Newgate, the Chaplain, often late at night. At the time Ikey Solomons was in Newgate, the Ordinary was the Reverend R. H. S. Cotton, and his notebook for part of the period has survived. Cotton agreed with the view that the Privy Council's decisions were unpredictable. He recorded on the 10th May, 1826, that two of the men reprieved 'seemed as though astonished that their lives were saved; particularly so, as by express orders from the Recorder they had been repeatedly told, while under sentence, that there appeared no hope of mercy for them'.

It is sometimes suggested that the uncertainty that the condemned prisoners had to endure, the anxious weeks of waiting, led to a high suicide rate. The surgeon's report enables us to say that this was not true, at any rate of the years at the end of the 1820s, the time when the Solomonses were passing through Newgate. Only one suicide attempt is recorded in a period over two years, and that an unsuccessful one. On 12th February, 1827, shortly before Ikey's arrest, a man named Pearse tried to kill himself shortly after he had left the court where he was convicted on a capital charge. He stabbed himself 'with a knife of considerable size in the region of the liver'. He figures in the sick reports as a patient in hospital for a number of weeks, being bled on a number of occasions, but despite this treatment he apparently survived. Another list of those convicted on charges bearing the death penalty bears out the view that very few committed suicide or died in Newgate from any cause—most were reprieved.

Cotton recorded faithfully his daily visits to the prison, paying particular attention to his ministrations to condemned men. The following entries are a fairly typical set of comments about a particular man.

'Friday 11th November, 1825. This evening the Recorder's Warrant arrived for the execution of Samuel Crooke on Wednesday next, for stealing in a Dwelling House—when I communicated the awful intelligence, he was greatly and properly affected—all the others who were respited, conducted themselves with great decorum.

12th November. Visited Samuel Crooke—there appeared no alteration in him—his mother and two sisters joined us at prayers in the condemned room . . . he desired to be attended by his own teacher, a Mr. Isaacs, a dissenter, which of course was readily granted.'

Crooke apparently was about twenty years old and had been a Sunday school teacher. The Ordinary visited him every day and recorded his reactions: 'His behaviour is well becoming his situation . . . he was not so depressed, but seemed more cheerful and expressed himself as having a good hope of salvation . . . found him very humble and resigned to his fate—he acknowledged the justice of his sentence, and seemed sensible of the enormity of his guilt. . . . Visited him again in the evening—he expressed his gratitude for the kindness that has been shown him in prison, and his perfect resignation; he said he entertained a good and assured hope through Christ, and of his acceptance hereafter—his teacher . . . had been with him most part of the day.'

The final entry was 'Wednesday, 16th November. The morning of the execution. . . . At his request I administered the

Sacrament, of which Sheriff Kelly and his nephew and the Reverend Mr. Collier, Mr. Isaacs and Mr. Baker were partakers— it was truly gratifying to see the Sheriff kneeling with the convict at the Holy Ordinance, and all seemed to receive comfort, however painful the circumstances.'

Cotton was indefatigable in his attempts to induce repentance and what was, by his standards, a proper frame of mind in the condemned men. One man had declared himself a deist, rather than a believer in any specific religion, and, notes Cotton, 'it struck me that the conversation of a sensible pious layman might by probability have more effect with him than that of a clergyman; accordingly a request was made to Alderman Brown—who while Sheriff, had been indefatigable in his attentions and religious assistance to the prisoners—and he kindly condescended to visit Cockerill—but it is to be feared with little success.' As has been seen in relation to Crooke, Cotton sometimes noted down remarks from prisoners expressing repentance and acceptance of their fate. He knew that these sentiments were not always genuine. On 3rd June, 1826, after describing the favourable results he had obtained by his ministrations to a condemned man, there appears the heartfelt cry 'Surely this cannot be deception—I say this because in circumstances of this kind we are very liable to be imposed upon, as experience has painfully taught.'

Six months later there was a sad incident, which seems to have impressed Cotton mainly because it too involved apparent deception by a prisoner and because a man being hanged did not peaceably accept his fate. On 1st January, 1827, a man named White, a prisoner of higher class than the majority, was being executed. White had earlier complained of the bad language of the others in the condemned cell and had been given favourable treatment. He had also been allowed not to have his hands tied in the ordinary way for the execution, and he took advantage of this fact. He had refused to have a cap placed over his eyes, 'and when the drop fell, he sprang up again and having partially released his hands, he seized the rope by which he was suspended, and remained in that position for some seconds, till the officers pushed him off—and thus he died (it is to be feared) in a very improper state of mind'. Whatever we may think of this incident today, we ought not to doubt the sincerity with which Cotton believed that the frame of mind in which White went to meet his Creator was more important than anything else.

Since 1783 the prisoners who were to die had been spared the journey through London to Tyburn, near Marble Arch, and executions took place outside Newgate itself. They were held in public, a practice which continued until 1868. Fashionable people would hire vantage points in buildings overlooking the scene and the general public would throng the streets to get a good view. In 1807, it was estimated that no less than 40,000 spectators were crammed into the area around the gallows. When Ikey Solomons was convicted for picking pockets in 1810, the offence had just ceased to be a capital one—the first victory of the reformers had been that in 1808 they had succeeded in having the punishment for picking pockets changed from death to transportation. However, long before that time it had been recognized that pickpockets seldom or never were hanged. From 1808 onwards the number of offences to which the death sentence was attached was steadily reduced and the number of people executed for offences other than murder similarly declined. Although 8,484 people were sentenced to death in England and Wales in the years 1828–34 only 355, or less than five per cent, were in fact executed. Between 1815 and 1829 the annual number of people executed for offences other than murder varied between thirty-five and ninety-seven; after 1829 the number of people hanged for offences other than murder decreased rapidly and after 1837 executions took place only for murder or attempted murder.

Condemned prisoners awaiting execution made up only a small part of the population of Newgate. The most numerous classes were those who had been convicted of felony and were awaiting transportation or disposal in other ways, or those who had been committed from the police courts of London or Middlesex on charges of felony and who were awaiting trial at the Old Bailey. There were also a number of debtors (until about 1815) and a few lunatics, and occasionally prisoners serving short sentences for contempt of court might be confined in the prison.

Other prisons in the metropolis catered for prisoners of different classes and, although we cannot be sure that Ikey Solomons was ever confined in any of them, it is reasonable to suppose that in the early states of his career, like so many others, he entered one or more of the lesser prisons of London. He might have spent some time in Middlesex House of Correction, at Coldbath Fields, near the Grays Inn Road. To this prison were sent adult males sentenced to short periods of imprisonment, as opposed to transportation. He might have been confined in the House of Correction in Tothill Fields, Westminster, where boys and women were kept. He might have been in the New Prison, Clerkenwell, which held prisoners on first arrest or when committed for questioning by magistrates of Middlesex, or in Horsemonger Lane Gaol, which served a similar purpose for the County of Surrey, or the City of London Bridewell, in Blackfriars. Certainly Ann Solomons spent a week in Clerkenwell in 1827. In all of these prisons, in Ikey's day, conditions were broadly similar to those which we have described for Newgate.

At the New Prison, Clerkenwell, the garnish paid to fellow prisoners was two bolts of beer. The gaoler charged a shilling for the first night and sixpence for every subsequent night for a bed in a single cell—otherwise the prisoner was put in the strong room, which was sixteen feet square. The fees at the prison for discharging a prisoner were four shillings and sixpence, with another shilling to the turnkey. People brought into the prison by the constables of the night and discharged by the Justices the next morning were charged two shillings. At the Giltspur Street Compter, a City of London prison which served a similar purpose, garnish had been abolished, but the entrance fee on the master's side was ten shillings and sixpence, and three shillings and sixpence a week was charged for bed, bedding and sheets. On the common side beds and bedding could be had for two shillings for the first night and one shilling for every subsequent night. Every night charge who was discharged by the magistrate in the morning had to pay three shillings and sixpence, and if he was committed for further examination before being discharged his payment rose to fourteen shillings and eight pence.

Acts of Parliament in 1823, 1825 and 1835, together with the work of the inspectors of prisons first appointed in the latter year, eventually brought about a change. The prisons under local control were by these acts made subject to national regulations, and the inspectors gradually managed to raise standards throughout the country. The reforming zeal of the early nineteenth century turned its rational and enquiring eye on many public institutions, and the prisons were no exception. The Utilitarians, followers of Jeremy Bentham and apostles of efficiency, sought to make prisons places where criminals earned their keep by useful work. The Evangelicals, active and earnest Christians, were more interested in reforming the wrongdoers by the power of religion. Both united in attacking the promiscuous squalor of the prisons of the day, and their influence helped the introduction of new methods. There was at this time a choice of system. Two new approaches to prison organization had begun in America, and they were hotly debated in England. In 1790 the Quakers of Pennsylvania had begun to keep prisoners in solitary confinement at the Walnut Street Prison, Philadelphia, and in 1818 the Western Penitentiary at Pittsburg was built specially for what had now become known as the solitary system. In this method of prison discipline, prisoners were kept apart from one another to prevent contamination and to make possible the silent reflection and prayer from which salvation would, it was thought, eventually come. In 1816 New York State began at Auburn its cheaper alternative, the silent system, where prisoners were kept in close association but where any attempt at communication between them brought an instant flogging. Both systems had supporters in England, although neither was adopted here in its full vigour. The solitary system of America became the separate system of England, the change of name being intended to bring out the point that prisoners, although cut off from other criminals, were not deprived of human contact but were regularly visited by the chaplain and the warders. The silent system in England did not have the fierceness of on-the-spot corporal punishment of the American jails. The introduction of these two methods in the 1830s meant that English prisons were transformed from those which Ikey Solomons had known. But by then he was far away in Australia.

In May, 1827, then, Ikey was once again in the prison in which he had been confined seventeen years previously. Although he was now safely lodged in Newgate, Ikey had a trick up his sleeve. He applied for bail, which in those days meant that he had to be taken from Newgate to the Court of King's Bench, in Westminster Hall, to appear before a judge. Prisoners in Ikey's situation obtained a bill of *habeas corpus*, which called for the gaoler to show cause for their detention, i.e., to produce the committal warrant. The judge could then release the prisoner on bail if he thought fit. A newspaper of the period makes the very plausible suggestion that Ikey's application for bail was made not with any hope of its being successful but merely as a means of promoting his escape. This may be the case, although the escape was made not on the first but on the second of two trips to Westminster—perhaps for some reason the projected escape could not be made on the first occasion. Ikey's application for bail was rejected and, whatever his motive, he can hardly have entertained very serious hopes of success. But on the way back to Newgate Ikey escaped from the coach in which he was making the journey.

There are a number of stories about the actual circumstances of the escape, which agree in broad outline. Solomons was escorted by two officers from the prison, Richard Smart, an under-gaoler with 17 years' experience, and a turnkey who bore the appropriate name of Key. A newspaper story says that Smart allowed Ikey's wife to accompany him inside the coach and his father-in-law to sit beside the coachman. The officers agreed that the coach should take a diversion in order to drop Mrs. Solomons in Petticoat Lane—which would represent a very considerable diversion from the direct route! When the door was opened in Petticoat Lane, the story goes on, Solomons himself jumped out, while a party of confederates slammed the door shut again in the face of the turnkeys and would not let them out until Ikey had made his escape down a side alley. Another story adds the improbable touch that Ikey snatched up a cup of coffee in a house in Petticoat Lane while dashing through it from front door to back! Another version says that Ikey's father-in-law was driving the coach himself, and that the turnkeys had rashly agreed to engage the coach which was standing at the head of a rank near a public house where they had stopped at Ikey's invitation. (It was not until many years later that Sherlock Holmes was to warn someone in similar circumstances not to take either the first or the second cab that presented itself!) In this version of the story, the officers had been given a drugged drink at the public house and had been unable to resist when the coach was driven to Petticoat Lane and Ikey made his escape. Another version is that Ikey was allowed to entertain the turnkeys at two pubs, the Magpie and the King of Prussia, and made his escape from the latter and not from a coach. When Ikey was eventually tried, Richard Smart gave his version of the story, which, not unnaturally, was rather more favourable from his point of view. Smart said that he had taken the prisoner from Newgate to the King's Bench and back one day, and to the King's Bench again on the next day, the day on which bail was rejected. Then, he said, there was a mob at the foot of Westminster Bridge, 'and I was afraid he would escape, so we took him into a public-house, to get rid of the mob; we had a glass of brandy and water—he wanted to go into the yard for a certain purpose: I took him out, brought him back into the room, and took some brandy and water which I found there; and when I brought him out I did not know what I was about, I was so giddy—I found I could not walk; a coach was called, and we got into it; it drove I do not know where—we got into Petticoat Lane, and he got away from me.'

The Keeper of Newgate's version of the escape was that 'the Hackney Coach into which they got in the Palace Yard, Westminster, has been since ascertained to have been owned and driven by Solomon's father-in-law, and under the pretext of making a call (which the Turnkeys improperly permitted) they went out of the road and upon the coach stopping the door was opened by a party of his friends and he was rescued from the custody of the Turnkeys.'

It was not unusual for prisoners to be moved from the courts to gaol in a hackney coach. Indeed, one of John Wontner's predecessors as Keeper of Newgate, J. A. Newman, had in 1813 complained to the Home Office of the burden that he had to bear in payment of coach hire (expenses of this sort had to be met by the Keeper out of his fees). 'It may be said (perhaps),' he wrote, 'that less expense in coach hire might be incurred if the Prisoners were to walk to Westminster and back again to Prison, but if that Expense was lessened, as great would be incurred by the necessity of my employing men to guard them: besides, the opportunities of Escape would be facilitated if the Prisoners were to walk through the crowded streets of the Metropolis . . . and of the two it appeared to me to be the cheapest as well as the safest way to convey them in Hackney Coaches.'

The two turnkeys who were with Ikey seem to have been very confident that they could look after him—they refused an offer of help from the tipstaff of the King's Bench (who was responsible for order in the court and the custody of prisoners awaiting a hearing), who was prepared to escort them back to Newgate with four of his men. Perhaps it was pride that made Smart and Key refuse this offer of assistance. They do not seem to have had any suspicions that an escape was to have been attempted; whichever version of the story is true, the officers clearly did not insist on a direct return to Newgate without stops or diversions. Perhaps they had been given a drugged drink, or just too much undrugged drink; perhaps Ikey told them some elaborate story to justify a diversion from the proper route—and maybe he gave them some money as a reward for their complaisance; perhaps they did not even realize that the coach had headed past Newgate into Whitechapel. But however it was managed, there is no doubt that Ikey managed to slip out of the coach and into the maze of streets and alleys around Petticoat Lane. On 25th May, 1827, Isaac Solomons escaped from custody.

Not unnaturally, the escape of so notorious a criminal created a stir in high places. On 26th May the Home Secretary wrote to the Lord Mayor of London, referring to Ikey's get-away and saying that it was 'highly necessary that immediate and strict enquiries should be made into the circumstances of this escape, and I have to request that you will investigate the conduct of the officers who permitted the escape of the prisoner, and I rely upon your Lordship and the Court of Aldermen taking such steps for punishing them and the other parties implicated in the escape as justice may require.' On the 31st May the Home Office received a letter from one of the sheriffs of the City of London, suggesting that Solomons would try to leave London on some vessel sailing from the river. In consequence, the Under-Secretary of State wrote to the magistrates of the Thames Police, saying that it was thought that 'Isaac Solomons who recently escaped from the custody of the Keeper of Newgate will attempt to quit this kingdom on board some vessel now setting out' and asking for 'directions for your officers to be vigilant in looking after the said person with a view to his being apprehended'. A letter to the Secretary of the Customs asked the Board of Customs to direct their officers to apprehend Solomons if he could be found, and a placard giving a description was enclosed. A handbill offered a £50 reward for capturing Isaac, giving his description. One of the constables of St. James's, Piccadilly, who knew him well, was called in by the Keeper of Newgate to help his attempt to recapture Solomons. However, despite handbills, descriptions, rewards, and special precautions, Isaac Solomons was not recaptured.

Ikey's escape had unfortunate consequences for a number of people associated with him. James Isaacs found himself under a suspicion of having participated in or countenanced Ikey's escape. On 28th May he went before the Lambeth Street magistrates and attempted to assure them of his complete innocence. 'We want to have nothing to do with you, Mr. Isaacs,' said Matthew Wyatt, one of the magistrates, 'you are not employed on any business that is now before us.' Isaacs unwisely persisted in his application and provoked Wyatt into saying 'We, as well as other people, have a right to exercise private opinion; it would be quite time enough to complain when any charge is advanced against you.' This led Isaacs to insist again that he had not 'lent

himself to any misrepresentations which might mislead the
Court'—at the time of the escape he had his witnesses all ready
for the bail application, his briefs prepared and four counsel
engaged. Even this did not help him: the magistrate scornfully
pointed out that these preparations could have been made to
disarm suspicion. 'I hesitate not to declare, that this escape is
most disgraceful to all persons directly or indirectly concerned in
it, with the exception, of course, of the criminal, whom no one
can possibly blame. . . . Nothing gives me more pleasure than
that it did not take place while Solomons was in the keeping of
our own officers, and that the one to whom the enormous and
seducing bribe of £1,000 was offered, had the spirit and integrity
to despise it.' Poor Isaacs was finally crushed by a question from a
lay magistrate, the Reverend Mr. Mathias, who was sitting with
the stipendiaries: 'Pray, Mr. Isaacs, do you think it at all probable
that the Court of King's Bench would admit Solomons to bail,
after knowing the number of extensive charges against him, and
hearing the depositions read over that were taken at this office?'
This was too much for him, and, according to *The Times*, 'To
this question, Mr. Isaacs made no reply, but took his departure,
requesting their worships to suspend their judgment on his
conduct until the result of an investigation that was about to
take place.'

The Lambeth Street magistrates had not heard the last of Ikey
Solomons or of James Isaacs. On 3rd June Ann Solomons applied
to the magistrates at Lambeth Street 'to solicit their assistance in
recovering from a person named Isaacs . . . a considerable sum of
money which he had received for his use, and which he now,
though having no claim on it either for services past or in prospect,
refused to deliver up'. The origin of this application was that
when Ikey was arrested he had had on him £180 in gold sovereigns and £45 in Bank of England notes. The magistrates had
held on to the money for a time, but the gold was of course
untraceable, and they had had to release that after the first couple
of examinations. But no-one claimed the bank-notes as having
been stolen from them (after all, people did not always keep a
record of the numbers of bank-notes) and when Ikey, after his

commitment to Newgate, claimed that he had no means with which to arrange his defence, the magistrates had ordered the money to be paid to Isaacs as Ikey's agent. Ann now sought to get the bank-notes. She explained that Ikey had received the sovereigns, 'but out of those, you will perceive, Isaacs has received £64 odd, and now, in addition, detains the £80 in notes. [The figure of £80 is hard to explain—the amount Ikey had on him is given earlier in this report and in a quite different account as being £45.] After my husband had got away, I called on him for the latter, but he refused peremptorily to give it to me, saying that his wife had £40, and he had the remainder, and I should not get a *skurrig* of it—these were his very words.' Ann's application was unsuccessful. John Hardwick, the magistrate, told her that the money had been paid at her husband's request to his accredited agent, and that her only remedy was an action for recovery of the money in the civil courts.

Isaacs was not the only one to suffer from Ikey's escape. Smart and Key, the two officers who were in charge of him, had to face an investigation at the Guildhall—which they seem to have survived without even being suspended. Some of those who had been injured by Ikey's criminal activities were further damaged by his escape. Sampson Copestake, one of those whose property had been found in Ikey's possession, applied in June to the Recorder at the Old Bailey sessions for the return of some of the property which was being held in connection with the charge. He had altogether lost property to the value of £400, and £100-worth was now in the custody of the court. He was allowed to have back all the goods not necessary for the prosecution, and on 28th September there were returned to him seventy-four pieces of cotton lace, eighty-eight caps, thirty lace collars, thirty-nine dozens of cap-crowns, 312 children's lace caps and twenty-seven pieces of bobbinet. It was not only his property that he had lost; he, like others, had had to hang around the Old Bailey until the sessions ended on 8th June, in case Ikey was recaptured. One of the prosecutors was from Liverpool and another from Huddersfield, and there were altogether fifty or sixty people involved as prosecutors or witnesses.

All had entered into recognisances to prosecute or give evidence against Ikey, and might have had to forfeit heavy sums of money if he had been forthcoming for trial during the sessions and they had not been present.

James Isaacs had been injured in his reputation by Isaac Solomons's escape, and others had had additional financial loss to add to what they had already suffered; but Ikey's family suffered more. Within a few months of his escape five members of his family had been arrested, one of them twice, and two of them were convicted of felony. One newspaper was led by this chain of events to exclaim that 'the hand of fate seems to rest heavily on the family of the Solomons', and some people might be tempted to think that the arrests are evidence of vindictiveness on the part of the authorities or of the police officers against the man whose escape had held officialdom up to ridicule. However, it seems more likely that what led to the arrests was primarily the officers' attention to Ikey's family in the hope of catching the escaped man himself—partly because of the reward, partly because of the kudos such a capture would attract.

There is no doubt that the first arrest of a member of Ikey's family was the result of a sharp eye being kept open for him by the police of London. On Tuesday, 19th June, 1827, at about ten-thirty p.m., as Richard Skillern, a conductor of the Bow Street Patrol, was taking his party down Bell Lane, Wentworth Street, he saw a cart drawn up at no. 12, Ikey's house. Two men were unloading mahogany furniture into the house. Not surprisingly, in view of the time of night, Skillern asked for an explanation, and when the men refused to give one he took them into custody. Mrs. Solomons came out of the house, and said that she had had the furniture for years, and the men then revealed that they had brought it round from Henry Street, Bedford Square, Commercial Road. Skillern left two men with Ann, 'who, as an indulgence, he did not remove, as she had a large family, and a sick child', and went round to Henry Street. He dashed into the house hoping to catch Ikey, but found the kitchen door open and the bed covers thrown back as if someone had 'hastily risen'. Perhaps he had just missed Ikey—and perhaps he was lucky to have missed him, for a loaded horse-pistol was under the pillow and a sword-cane lying by the bed. These events gave the patrol the right to search the houses in Bell Lane and in Henry Street, and they found stolen property worth £4,000–5,000. Ann was arrested, and on 20th June she appeared again before Wyatt and Hardwick at Lambeth Street, this time charged with receiving stolen goods.

'When placed at the bar,' recorded *The Times*, 'Mrs. Solomons appeared much agitated and dejected, and during the examination the tears rapidly chased each other down her cheeks.' Although Wyatt knew that whatever sum he set as bail would be produced —'£50,000 if demanded'—he would not allow Ann's release: 'to do so would be a crime against society, and, as in the late occurrence (we believe [said *The Times* cautiously] he meant the escape of Solomons), defeat the end of justice.' Ann was sent to the New Prison, Clerkenwell, pending further examination.

A week later, on Wednesday, 27th June, Ann appeared in court again. 'When placed in the dock, a strong feeling of shame seemed to influence her. She held down her head, during the time of her detention, and appeared much depressed, and fearful of looking in the face of anyone.' Many people had been to look at the stolen property, but identification had proved difficult because the marks had been removed from the goods, and even the basting threads taken out of the made-up garments. However, members of the firm of Davis & Co. were able to identify some waistcoats, as the valencia of which they were made was of a distinctive pattern used only in goods stolen from Friday Street, Cheapside, some three years previously; they were valued at £400. The magistrate pointed out that the goods could have come honestly into Ikey's possession during the period between theft and discovery; in any event, Ann could not be held responsible for property found in her husband's house which her husband could have brought there. The lapse of time was decisive: as Ikey had been arrested in May, 1827, his wife was not answerable for the presence in his house of property which was stolen before that date, unless it could in some way be proved that the property was not there until after Ikey's arrest. The law

G

assumed that a wife was obedient to the orders of her husband—
it was this assumption, it will be remembered, that provoked
Mr. Bumble to say that the law is 'a ass, a idiot'—and Ann could
thus only be held responsible for acts committed after Ikey's
arrest. She was accordingly discharged. However, the magistrates
ordered that all the property should be retained, cynically
observing that 'not one article should be given up until Mr.
Solomons came and lawfully claimed it'.

Two days later, on Friday evening, John Solomons, the eldest
son of Ikey and Ann, was arrested by Skillern at the Henry Street
house. Ann Solomons was not at the house at the time, the only
other occupants being 'a little boy and girl'—probably David
and Anne Solomons, aged respectively nine and seven, thus
making an early acquaintanceship with the police. John, 'a young
man of perfectly good appearance, as yet in his minority',
appeared at Lambeth Street on Saturday, 30th June, charged
with receiving the stolen property. It now transpired that the
Henry Street house had only recently been rented by the Solomonses, and that it was John who had negotiated the lease. It was
alleged that John had taken the house in a fictitious name, which
would have been evidence supporting the suggestion that he
knew stolen property was to be kept there. However, his solicitor
argued that 'Sloman', the name which was used, was the way in
which 'Solomon' was often pronounced and spelled. James Paris,
the landlord of the house, a publican, gave evidence that John
had first given his name as Isaac Sloman, then corrected it to
John. He had given the impression that he had taken the house
for his father—when the rent was agreed, he had said that he would
go to Highgate to collect it. A quarter's rent had been paid in
advance, at the rate of £26.15.0 a year; and Paris was reprimanded by the magistrates for negligence in letting his house in
these suspicious circumstances. However, the magistrates felt that
there was insufficient evidence against John Solomons, and he
was discharged.

Less than a week later, on Friday, 6th July, John's grandfather
was arrested. This was again clearly the result of Ikey's escape.
When William Wadham Cope, Under Marshal of the City of

London and one of its leading professional policemen, heard of Ikey's escape he, doubtless like most other police officers in London, went into action at once. With some of his men he 'went to search all the places where they thought it was possible the fugitive might be concealed. It has been a practice with knowing thieves of late, to hide, when they know that they are "wanted", in the very spots where a person would never think of looking for them—namely, in their own, or their relations' houses.' Cope accordingly went to Ikey's father's house, 24 Gravel Lane, Houndsditch, at five o'clock in the afternoon of the escape, 'determined to ransack every part of the habitation'. The only person in the house was Ikey's mother, but Cope found some valuable property, including a box containing six gold and eleven silver watches. He took the goods to the Mansion House and the Lord Mayor ordered that they should be advertised as suspected stolen property. A warrant was issued for the arrest of Henry Solomons, Ikey's father.

The watches and other valuables were promptly identified: on 26th May they were seen by George Grant, a watchmaker and jeweller of 21 Chancery Lane, who claimed them as property stolen from him on the night of 24th–25th May. The police officers accordingly kept a look-out for Henry Solomons, and on Friday, 6th July, at about seven-fifteen p.m., he was arrested—Vann, a member of the Bow Street Patrol, had spotted him in South London. On 7th July Henry appeared before the Lord Mayor at the Mansion House. His solicitor reserved his defence, although he said he had a complete answer to the charge, and Henry was committed to be tried at the Old Bailey. He was taken on the same day to Newgate, where he gave his age as sixty-nine and his occupation as 'dealer'—a vague expression which his son had also used. Henry was five feet high, stoutish in build. His complexion was ruddy, his hair grey, and his eyes hazel; he had been born at Wurzburg, in Bavaria.

On 14th July Henry Solomons stood his trial before the Recorder of the City of London. He was indicted for stealing on the 25th May: '27 watches value £114, 7 pairs of earrings value £2.10.0, 7 brooches value £25, 14 watch-keys value £4,

14 seals value £16, 28 rings value £25, 5 watch chains value
£24, 8 shirt pins value £1, 2 eyeglasses value £1, 2 pairs of
bracelet snaps value 14s. and 1 locket value 4s. 6d., the goods of
George Grant.' Grant gave evidence that the goods had been
stolen from him, Cope that he had found them in Henry
Solomons's house the next day. Vann described his arrest of
Solomons, which had been the result of pure chance—he had
recognized him in the street. The defence suggested that Vann
had tried to get Solomons to buy him a drink or to give him
money. The story might well have been true, although Henry
would have had to pay a high price to persuade Vann to give
up so famous a prize. But of course Vann denied the suggestion
hotly. Vann testified at the trial that on being charged the
prisoner had said that the box of stolen property would have
been too heavy for him to carry—'Oh he could not carry such
things, that they were brought there by his son.' To block his
attempt to put the blame on Ikey, John Wontner, the Keeper
of Newgate, gave evidence of the time of Ikey's escape, and
swore that he could not have been in Chancery Lane at the time
Grant's shop was broken into. He added that by the Lord Mayor's
order Henry had been kept in the infirmary whilst in Newgate—
Henry had complained about his health.

Henry's defence was a complete denial: 'I am upwards of
seventy years old, and have worked hard to support my family.
I never got a penny dishonestly in all my days—I have worked
for every factory in London. I hate the very thoughts of a thief
and of a receiver. . . . I have been ill upwards of three years, and
cannot get out of bed without by my wife or daughter putting
my stockings on—having had a hurt across my loins.' Sarah
Nathan, his widowed daughter, gave supporting evidence. Her
father was an ailing man, seldom or never well. She had lived
with him for the past five years, taking care of him and her
mother, who was seventy-three years old. The family were not
on good terms with Ikey. Her father, she said, usually worked at
home and was a glass engraver—she would not have known that
he had described himself as a dealer to the authorities of Newgate.
She too put the blame for the stolen property on Ikey. On 25th

May, between twelve noon and one p.m., 'a lad brought this locked box to the house', and said he left it for Isaac Solomons. 'We were not friends with my brother,' she said—Ikey was not on good terms with the rest of the family. One shrewd question was put to Sarah in cross-examination: if her father was so ill, how had he managed to walk to the spot in South London where he had been arrested, the Obelisk in St. George's Circus, at the junction of Borough Road and Waterloo Road, over a mile from London Bridge and further still from Gravel Lane? Unfortunately her answer is not recorded! Despite Sarah's evidence, despite five witnesses who testified to his good character, Henry Solomons was found guilty of the theft. He was also charged with stealing 'a silver teapot valued at £4', the property of Francis Hale Rigby, but this case was not tried and the indictment was left on the file. Sentence was, however, not passed on him at the end of the sessions; judgment was respited until the next sessions. This happened in a few cases in each sessions, and his age and alleged ill-health may have been the explanation. Certainly, when on 23rd September sentence of six months' detention in the House of Correction was announced, Henry 'was informed, that in consequence of his great age, that mild sentence was passed on him'. The next day he was transferred from Newgate to a 'House of Correction', although we do not know which one. As the six months counted from the time of his conviction in July, he had already served more than a third of his time.

Thus Ikey's wife, son and father had been arrested within two months of his escape, and his father was now a convicted felon. Worse was soon to befall the family, however. Ann was soon arrested again, and this time was unable to shift the blame on to her husband; she was tried and convicted. Her second son Moses was arrested with her, but was soon released.

Before describing these events, however, it will be convenient to jump ahead a few months to mention the arrest of the fifth member of the Solomons family. On 24th October, 1827, Benjamin Solomons, Ikey's brother, appeared before the Lord Mayor at the Mansion House, charged with receiving stolen property. John Goulding of the Bow Street Patrol had found in Benjamin's house in Petticoat Lane some property which he believed to have been stolen from a church. He was not able to say which church it was stolen from, a fact which weakened his case and which James Isaacs, appearing for Benjamin, quite correctly drew to the attention of the court. It is not clear how Goulding acquired his right to search Benjamin's house—some grounds for suspicion must have existed, however, as Isaacs did not challenge him on this point. The Lord Mayor remanded the prisoner for further enquiries—that is to say, for Goulding to try to find someone who would identify the suspect property. Isaacs applied for bail, but this was refused and Benjamin was sent to the Compter, one of the City's lock-ups for short-stay prisoners. On 28th October Benjamin re-appeared in court. The patrol had no evidence to offer on the receiving charge; evidently no one had come forward to claim the property. Goulding asked for the further detention of the prisoner 'as his wife had not been able to account for a watch which fell from her person', but this improper request was rejected and Benjamin was immediately discharged. He left the court threatening to sue Goulding for wrongful arrest.

Thus the Solomons family had had mixed success in their encounters with the law in 1827. Ikey had made good his escape, and John, Moses and Benjamin had been discharged at the magistrates' court. But Henry had been convicted, although his sentence had been a light one. Ann Solomons had escaped unharmed in her first encounter with the law, being discharged after a week or so in custody; but her second arrest was to lead to the wholesale removal of the family of Ikey Solomons from London to Australia.

Chapter Five

ANN SOLOMONS

Ann Solomons carried on the family business after Isaac's arrest and subsequent escape. When she was arrested in June, 1827, the officers were not able to identify any of the property they found as having been stolen after Ikey's arrest, and thus it was not possible to convict her of receiving; but it was not long before the circumstances changed.

On 29th August, 1827, at seven-thirty in the morning, William Brown Edwards, a police officer from the Hatton Garden Office, appeared at the Solomonses' house in Bell Lane with a search warrant. The warrant, issued at the request of the authorities of the Royal Mint, authorized him to search for counterfeit money. The hunt went on until 10 a.m., by which time Edwards and his companions had found 554 base sovereigns, but what was to prove much more important was the mass of ill-acquired property which they found in the house as well. The search was a thorough one—the whole of the yard was dug up, and the officers pulled up the floor-boards on the ground floor, finding some property which had been concealed under a trap-door. Ann tried to take advantage of the fact that the goods were hidden so thoroughly to claim that she knew nothing of them and that her husband must have left them there—but as one of the watches found under the floor was actually going at the time, the officers did not feel inclined to believe her story!

The stolen property was not all under the floor-boards, and the officers found 'an immense quantity of jewellery, consisting of gold and silver watches, trinkets of great value, gold rings, etc., together with other property, such as lace, silks, and crapes'. Two coach-loads were taken by the officers on their first visit, and two further visits had to be made to complete the task. The property was displayed at Hatton Garden Police Office for identification, and it was said that the place was 'a complete Bazaar'. At least twenty respectable tradesmen called within the first hour to see if they could identify their property, and John Limbrick, one of the officers who had searched Ann's house, 'took every pain to gratify the wishes of the various visitants'. The goods were in such a confusion that it was difficult to make a proper search, and another day was fixed for inspection, 'against which time the goods were to be arranged in regular order'. However, some of the property was identified on the first day, and before long three charges of receiving stolen property were brought against Ann.

Ann had been arrested on the day of the search, in company with her second son Moses, who was then seventeen or eighteen years old, and Clara Brown her servant girl, aged about twenty-one. (John, the eldest son, was said by Ann to be in America or on his way back from that country, although it was only two months since he had been released from custody at Lambeth Street.) 'Several respectably dressed persons of the Jewish persuasion' went to Hatton Garden Police Office and asked for permission to interview Ann, but they were not allowed to do so. However, her sister was allowed to see her, in the presence of one of the officers, to make arrangements for the care of her infant child, Mark, who was about a year old.

The three accused appeared before the magistrate at Hatton Garden on 4th September, and again on 12th September. On this latter occasion, the case was heard in full. The son and the servant were discharged, but Ann was committed by Mr. Serjeant Sellon to stand her trial on four charges—three charges of receiving stolen goods and one of receiving 540 counterfeit sovereigns with intent to circulate them. Ironically enough, this latter charge, the one that had led to the fatal search of Ann's house, was not proceeded with.

Ann was very soon in the dock at the Old Bailey. The first day fixed for the trial was 18th September, less than a week after the committal. On that day, declared the *Morning Post*, 'every avenue leading to the court was thronged with persons of the Jewish persuasion'. There was, however, little for them to hear, for Ann's counsel was granted a postponement of two days to complete the preparation of her defence. The trial thus took place on 20th September. Mr. Brodrick defended Ann, with Mr. Law; Mr. Adolphus, who had been briefed to defend Ikey before his escape, appeared for the prosecution. The first of the three indictments accused Ann of receiving from 'a certain evil disposed person' the watch of Joseph Ridley, value £6, which 'had been lately before (by the said evil disposed person), feloniously stolen, she well knowing the same to have been stolen'. Joseph Ridley, a ship's captain, gave evidence that on 17th August, while he 'was not perfectly sober', the watch was stolen from him somewhere in Whitechapel. He reported the loss to the Lambeth Street Office on 20th August. When the officers searched Ann's house on 29th August, they found the watch, which was duly identified by Ridley. Ann could offer no excuse for possessing something which had so recently been stolen, and she was found guilty. The two other charges concerned property which had been stolen some time before. One concerned a watch which had been stolen in December, 1826, the other some cloth and waistcoats stolen two-and-a-half years previously. These charges, like those brought against Ann in June, collapsed when it was shown that Ikey was still at large after the goods were stolen, and hence the blame could not be put at Ann's door. She was consequently acquitted on the two latter charges.

On 23rd September Ann returned to the court to receive her sentence. Her father-in-law, whose case had been postponed from the previous sessions, was there as well for the same purpose. Ann was not as lucky as Henry Solomons. Seeming, according to a newspaper report, 'much agitated', she was sentenced to fourteen years' transportation. 'The appearance of Mrs. Solomons,' recorded the *Morning Chronicle*, 'seemed to excite the most intense interest. She was most elegantly dressed. On hearing the sentence she fainted, but recovered before she left the dock, and exclaimed, as she was leaving the Court, "Oh, my poor children— my poor children".'

Ann Solomons did not lie down quietly under her conviction. She petitioned the King for the right, which was granted to some people, to 'transport herself out of the kingdom'—to leave the country for the period of her sentence, but to do so as a free person travelling under her own arrangements, without the ignominy and discomfort of movement as a convict. To justify her request, she told a harrowing tale. She declared that she was 'deeply impressed with shame and sorrow under her present most distressing, painful, and unfortunate situation'. Her petition continued: 'She is a poor, weak Woman, led astray from the paths of rectitude by others. That at the moment she was making speedy preparations for quitting for ever her Native Country, she was led by a certain party, to receive the beforementioned watch into her possession; the duty of which party ought rather to have advised her against such a measure, and not have led her into her present heavy troubles and misfortunes, which at last they were only enabled to do by their most pressing and long solicitations, and which in the end unfortunately proved too powerful for the weakness of her nature to withstand. But who was this party? Her brother-in-law Benjamin Solomon, who had previously laid this plan for entrapping your unfortunate and distracted prisoner, for the purpose, or as a means thereby, of procuring his father Henry Solomon's liberty; and who has in consequence had a mitigated sentence of six months imprisonment.' Ann then talks of her six children, one still an infant, and her problems since her husband left the country, and asks to be allowed to transport herself with all her children. 'And as in most sincere gratitude and humble duty your petitioner, a miserable woman—a distracted mother will ever be bound to pray, etc, etc.' (This last phrase is the formal ending of all petitions, what the petitioner was bound to pray *for* having long ceased to be stated in actual words!)

Ann and her friends had been sufficiently active to win over to her side Joseph Ridley, the prosecutor, whose watch was the source of all Ann's troubles. Joseph Ridley, too, petitioned the King. 'Your petitioner having heard numerous reports in favour of Ann Solomon since her conviction, felt it his duty to use every means in his power to ascertain the truth thereof, and after the most minute investigations in quarters very respectable, your petitioner has learnt that the unfortunate woman has been altogether the victim of a bad connection, having been basely tempted and betrayed, by those who ought to have protected her. That your petitioner since this discovery feels most deeply interested in her favour, and humbly hopes that Your Majesty may be most graciously pleased to grant her the prayer of her annexed petition.'

The cynical may perhaps believe that some means had been found to enlist Joseph Ridley's sympathy on Ann's behalf. Ridley certainly was anxious about Ann, for with the petitions already quoted there is, filed in the Public Record Office, another one from him, saying that he had petitioned the King on behalf of Ann Solomons 'about eight days since but has not received any reply'. The second petition was even more pressing than the first. Ridley 'humbly begged leave to represent to Your Most Gracious Majesty that he has again made every enquiry into this poor woman's case and finds she was completely trepanned into her present distressing condition by her brother-in-law in order to exonerate his father who was confined at the time under suspicious circumstances. That your petitioner has every reason to believe that the watch found in the possession of Ann Solomon was the only article bought since her husband left the country, and that she would not have purchased the same had she not been over-persuaded by her brother-in-law for the beforementioned reason.' Ridley then, perhaps unwisely, pointed out that it was not unusual for the request which he made to be granted—'Your Most Gracious Majesty has been pleased to extend your goodness to several persons similarly situated, and allow them the indulgence of transporting themselves beyond the seas.' As he found that 'the unfortunate woman's conduct' was 'very favourable', he hoped that the King, as it was her first offence, would allow her the same indulgence. Alas for Ridley's hopes and for Ann's, the petitions are marked simply 'Nil January 8th 1828'. Ann Solomons's fate had been sealed, and she was to be transported beyond the seas.

Ikey Solomons also spoke of this alleged plot against his wife in a petition which he himself submitted to the Home Secretary when in Newgate in 1830. He described the way in which 'an innocent Woman and helpless Family' had been 'plunged into despair, through the malicious artifices and designs of my own Relations'. He explained how it happened. 'While in America I wrote to my Wife requesting her to purchase a few watches and send them to me as I had been in the habit of dealing in that line for many years.' This remark, it may be noted, disclosed a certain coolness, as at the time when Ikey wrote this petition he had been convicted of receiving stolen watches! Ikey alleged that his wife then asked various people, including two of his own relations, to assist her, and they 'took advantage of that intimation and hence arose an opportunity of putting their base designs into effect. In compliance with my request she purchased a few of the Articles above named and amongst them was one which proved her destruction.' It is not possible to say whether there was any justification for the accusation which Ikey and his wife made against his relations. There is certainly no reason to seek any explanation other than his age for Henry's sentence, nor is there any evidence that he did not serve his imprisonment in the usual way. Be that as it may, at least we can say that the Solomons family were reasonably consistent in their allegations, even after a period of time and after many adventures.

Whether or not it was due to the machinations of her relations, Ann Solomons was now in Newgate, awaiting transportation to Australia. Women convicts were not sent to the hulks, but remained in Newgate until their release or their shipment to Australia. Women sentenced to transportation stood a much higher chance than the men who were in the same predicament of actually being sent to Australia. This was especially true around the time when Ann was convicted, when the government increased the number of ships carrying women convicts to Australia, in order to increase the female population there.

At a time when conditions for all prisoners were extremely harsh, certainly by our standards and even by the standards of many people at the time, the lot of a woman prisoner was not a

comfortable one. However, by the time Ann arrived in Newgate
the situation was a great deal better than it had been at the
beginning of the century. The improvement had begun in 1817,
when Elizabeth Fry started her school in Newgate. Mrs. Fry
and her brothers-in-law, Samuel Hoare and Thomas Fowell
Buxton, were active prison reformers, and they helped to
establish the Society for the Reformation of Prison Discipline
in 1816. By that time the three of them had visited a number of
prisons in London and elsewhere, and Elizabeth had made
frequent calls at Newgate in the year 1813, helping to clothe
the children and the sick. In 1817, however, Elizabeth Fry
embarked in real earnest on her work in Newgate, the work that
she was to continue until her death in 1843 and that has made her
world-famous.

When Mrs. Fry first visited Newgate in 1813, she found
nearly 300 women, some untried, some under sentence of death,
crowded together in a small space, cooking, washing, eating and
sleeping all in the same room, with very little bedding or clothing.
When she took up her regular work in 1817 she managed to
win the support of the women prisoners for the idea that there
should be a school in Newgate for the children of prisoners and
for juvenile criminals. She managed also to perform the more
difficult task of winning the support of the authorities of the
prison—the Governor of Newgate, the two Sheriffs of London,
and the Ordinary (the Chaplain) of the prison. Mrs. Fry recorded
in her diary: 'I have lately been much occupied in forming a
school in Newgate for the children of the poor prisoners, as well
as the young criminals, which has brought much peace and
satisfaction with it.' Thirty pupils, mostly seven years old or
younger, were enrolled in the school. However, many of the
older girls, and even grown women, begged and pleaded to be
allowed to attend the school, or to be given work to end the
enforced idleness of prison. These requests led Mrs. Fry to take
her scheme a stage further and do something for the women
prisoners. She formed a body known as the Ladies' Association
for the Improvement of the Female Prisoners in Newgate, usually
called the Ladies' Newgate Committee. The members of the

committee promised to take turns to go daily to the prison, to instruct the women in needlework and supervise their activities, to provide the materals and arrange for the sale of the finished articles. The women made 'caps, dressing gowns, baby-linen, bags, rugs, patch-work, counterpanes of elegant designs, etc.'. The Committee also paid the salary of a matron, who lived in the prison. The prisoners agreed to the rules proposed by Mrs. Fry and her friends. They were divided into groups of not more than twelve, with a monitor over each, to check the work and to keep an account of the amount earned. There were about seventy of them, aged from eighteen to sixty, in the group as a whole. A visitor described what he had seen: 'I was conducted by a decently dressed person, the newly-appointed yards-woman, to the door of a ward, where, at the head of a long table, sat a lady belonging to the Society of Friends. She was reading aloud to about sixteen women prisoners, who were engaged in needle-work around it. Each wore a clean-looking blue apron and bib, with a ticket having a number on it suspended from her neck by a red tape . . . their countenances wore an air of self-respect and gravity.'

The Grand Jury of the City of London, which shared with the Grand Jury of Middlesex the duty of reporting on conditions in the prison, in 1818 recorded, 'They cannot conclude their report except by expressing in an especial manner the peculiar gratification they experience in observing the important service rendered by Mrs. Fry and her friends, and the habits of religion, order, industry and cleanliness which her humane, benevolent and praiseworthy exertions have introduced amongst the female prisoners; and that if the principles which govern her regulations were adopted towards the males, as well as the females, it would be the means of converting a prison into a school of reform; and instead of sending criminals back into the world hardened in vice and depravity, they would be restored to it repentant, and probably become useful members of society.' Although the hopes of the Grand Jury were not by any means fulfilled, the general tone of the prison had improved by the time of Ann's visit ten years after this comment was made.

An important part of Elizabeth Fry's work in Newgate was her care for the women prisoners who were about to be transported. This began when one day she found on her arrival at Newgate that the turnkeys were preparing for a night of riot. They explained to her that some of the women were to be taken to a convict-ship the next morning, and that there was always a riot in the prison on the night before such an event. The women all 'went mad', got drunk and tore things up, broke and set fire to everything they could, and fought vigorously. (It may be noted that outbreaks of hysteria, with damage to property, are known to occur in women's prisons even in the present day.) The turnkeys spoke with reluctance of the problem which they would as usual face, of putting irons on the women who were to be shipped to Australia in order to be able to load them into the wagons which were to take them down to the ship. Mrs. Fry decided to try another approach. She obtained official authority to make personally all the arrangements for the removal of the prisoners to the ship, and got agreement that they should not be ironed and that they should travel in closed hackney-coaches and not open wagons. She spent the evening with the women in Newgate, reading to them and helping them to face the future with as much confidence as was possible. She promised to go with them right to the ship the next morning. Instead of the usual night of riot and debauchery, it was an occasion of prayer and sad farewells. The women who were remaining in Newgate made a collection for those who were to go to Australia, and urged them to take the money as a contribution to help deal with all the difficulties of the journey.

The next morning Mrs. Fry, with some of the ladies of the committee, was at the prison in time to arrange for the transfer of the women who were to be sent to Australia; they helped them into the coaches and went with them as they drove to the convict-ship *Maria I*. One hundred and twenty-six women convicts were loaded on board this ship and taken to Sydney, New South Wales, two of them dying on the journey.

The vessel sailed in May, 1818, but it lay in the river six weeks after the women from Newgate had been put aboard. Mrs. Fry visited the ship regularly, talking not only to those from Newgate but also to the other women who came down in dribs and drabs from the other prisons of the country. Eventually she established her dominance over all of them, and persuaded them to organize themselves on the pattern she had introduced in Newgate. The women were divided into classes of twelve, and each class had its monitor. Each of the women was given a number; this was for their own satisfaction and not for any official purpose. The women liked the idea of being numbered because it made it easier for them to keep their own seats at table and to keep their private possessions to themselves. Each of the classes was provided with materials for patchwork. Mrs. Fry had even arranged a school for the fourteen children on board the ship, and selected one of the prisoners to act as schoolmistress. As she left them on the day on which they were to sail, one of the prisoners leaned over the side of the vessel and said to her, 'Our prayers will be for you, and a convict's prayers will be heard.'

From that time onwards Mrs. Fry visited every convict-ship carrying women prisoners to the colonies until she died in 1843. She introduced into every one of them her system of organization. In all, 106 ships and some 12,000 convicts on board them benefitted from her activities. She soon was able to obtain from government a regulation prohibiting the ironing of women prisoners on their journey from prison to convict-ship—on one occasion she had seen a party of eleven arrive with iron bands round legs and arms chaining them all together. Mrs. Fry was instrumental in obtaining regulations that women convicts could take with them all their children under the age of seven, as Ann Solomons was to do, and that the mother of a nursing baby should not be embarked on board a convict-ship until the child was weaned.

She and her Ladies' Committee gave supplies to each prisoner: 'One Bible, one hessian apron, one black stuff ditto, one black cotton cap, one black hessian bag (to keep her clothes in); one small bag containing one piece of cake, one ounce of pins, one hundred needles, four balls of white sewing cotton, one ditto black, one ditto blue, one ditto red, two balls of black worsted, twenty-four hanks of coloured thread, one of cloth with eight darning-needles, one small bodkin fastened on it; two stay-laces, one thimble, one pair of scissors, one pair of spectacles when required, two pounds of patchwork pieces, one comb, one small ditto, knife and fork, and a ball of string.' Each prisoner's gifts were marked with her own number for the voyage, to avoid any disputes; a set was made ready for each ship as it was filled with women prisoners. The patchworking was not merely to keep the women active while on their journey. The ships en route to Australia often touched at Rio de Janeiro, and it was quite often possible to sell a patchwork quilt there for a guinea. But if they could not be sold at Rio, they could be sold immediately on arrival at Sydney or Hobart, and the women would thus have ready money on their arrival in the colony, and, what was perhaps more important, a reputation for industry and a trade already to hand. The Ladies' Committee also provided books for the women on the convict-ships. 'The library,' wrote one observer, 'was of great use, as it was only on condition of good conduct that they were allowed to have a book . . . it was very pleasant to see here and there a group seated listening to one of their companions reading aloud.' Mrs. Fry was a Quaker, and therefore we must not be too surprised to learn that the books were carefully selected, and that all 'novels, plays and other improper books' were excluded; the women had to content themselves with travel, biography, history, serious poetry and religious works.

One of the women to benefit from Mrs. Fry's work was Mrs. Ikey Solomons. Ann had not had to spend long waiting to begin her journey halfway round the world. The first news she had that she was about to be sent to Australia may have been on 21st January, 1828, when the surgeon of the convict-ship went to Newgate to examine the women it was intended to entrust to his care. He passed ninety-five of the ninety-eight on the list, and eight days later he called again and passed two of the remaining three, who had 'improved in health' in the interim. So by 29th January at the latest Ann Solomons knew her fate. On 24th

H

February she sailed from London in the *Mermaid*, arriving in Van Diemen's Land on 27th June.

The idea of sending criminals out of the country already had a long history by Ann's day. Parliament first gave authority for wrongdoers to be sent overseas in Tudor days, and during the latter part of the seventeenth and the early part of the eighteenth century the system was extended. Until the American Revolution, transportation to the colonies in the New World was an important way of disposing of criminals. Some people were sentenced to transportation as a penalty for minor offences, and in many cases a death sentence passed for a more serious offence was commuted to transportation. Convicts on arrival in America had to work for a specified number of years for a settler who had bought their services from the government (through the contractor who shipped them out), but their situation was often no worse than that of free labourers who had entered into a bond to work for a number of years in America as a means of paying the cost of their passages. None the less, the system of transporting convicts was unpopular with the legislatures of the American colonies. Such was the shortage of labour, however, and so great were the advantages of the system to many of the people of the colonies, that the legislators were not able to persuade the home government to end the practice. But after the stirrings of revolt in 1775 it was no longer possible to send English or Irish convicts to America.

The first alternative to the American colonies as a means of disposing of convicts, the temporary expedient which was all that was thought necessary, was to moor the hulks of disused warships on the River Thames or elsewhere, and to put convicts in them. The hulks system has been described more fully in an earlier chapter, and it is enough to note here that the temporary expedient which was authorized for two years in 1776 in fact lasted for eighty-two years. None the less, it proved inadequate. In 1778 it was noted that the hulks were supposed to hold only 380 convicts, but that before the American War of Independence nearly a thousand people had been shipped to the colonies every year. Committees of the House of Commons which looked into

the problem were full of suggestions for shipping the convicts
off to other parts of the world. 'Transportation to unhealthy
places,' said one of them, 'in place of sending better citizens,
may be advisable.' Various parts of Africa were being considered,
but one suggestion to this committee, although disregarded at
the time, was later to be fruitful. Sir Joseph Banks, the naturalist,
explorer and benefactor of the British Museum, gave evidence
to the committee. He had accompanied Captain Cook in his
voyage round the world on the *Endeavour* in the years 1768–71,
and he now suggested that Botany Bay, on the south-eastern
shore of Australia, might be a suitable place for a convict settlement. For the time being, however, nothing was done. The
government seemed to favour settlements in Africa, but all the
suggested sites eventually proved unsatisfactory. In the end, in
1785 it was decided to found a penal settlement at Botany Bay.

What is known in Australian history as the First Fleet set out
from Spithead on 13th May, 1787, carrying 568 male and 191
female prisoners. The Fleet arrived in Botany Bay in January,
1788, but the prisoners were not landed there. Within a week
of the arrival Arthur Phillip, the naval officer who was the first
Governor of Australia, realized that Sydney Cove, a few miles
to the north of Botany Bay, was a far better site, and moved the
entire fleet there. Thus there never was a convict settlement at
Botany Bay—yet for fifty years or more 'Botany Bay' was the
name given by the criminals of London to the place where
they expected to end their days.

The life of the early settlers of Australia, convict or free, was
not an easy one. It had been planned that the settlement should
become self-supporting in food and in the basic necessities of
life within a very short space of time, but this soon proved to
be a vain hope. Governor Phillip reported: 'No country offers
less assistance to the first settlers than this does, nor do I think
that any country could be more disadvantageously placed with
respect to support from the Mother Country on which for a
few years we must entirely depend.' It proved very difficult to
produce enough food for everyone in the early years, and every
ship arriving from England brought new mouths to feed as

further convicts and free settlers came to Australia. Supplies of all kinds were short, and prices high.

The new settlement faced entirely new problems. In America the convicts had been handed over to their masters by the private contractors who had carried them to the colonies. In Australia the convicts remained throughout in official hands. Their movement overseas was arranged by the home government, and on arrival the convicts passed into the control of the Governor of the colony. Many of them were employed on public works of one kind or another. However, some convicts were assigned by the government to work for individual settlers. Some of the officers of the government had obtained grants of land, and they were each entitled to have the services of ten convicts to help cultivate it. Some of the 'more deserving' of the free settlers were also assigned servants from amongst the convicts, particularly if they took on the obligation of feeding them and thus saved government supplies. As private farming spread, so the number of assigned convicts increased. Other convicts, usually as a reward for good conduct, were given a 'ticket of leave', which excused them from working for the government or for anyone else, and allowed them to earn their own living—another way of relieving government of the obligation to feed them. They could work as carpenters, tailors, or shoe makers, they could make cloth and hats, or work in the breweries, fisheries, and other growing trades of the colony. The Governor reported in 1809: 'The exertions of the whole Colony are not now, as formerly, solely directed to agriculture.' In 1809 Colonel Lachlan Macquarie became Governor of New South Wales, and his tour of office, ending in 1821, saw the transformation of the territory from a mere penal settlement to a flourishing colony. The introduction of sheep, associated above all with the name of John Macarthur, had provided the colony with what was to be a major source of income.

The very fact that New South Wales had now become a colony which was attractive to free settlers had made it less suitable for use as a penal settlement, although convicts continued to be sent there in large numbers until 1840. The Governor

of New South Wales had in 1803 sent a party of convicts to
establish a settlement in Van Diemen's Land, the modern Tasmania, and another settlement was formed on the island in the
following year. Thereafter increasing numbers of convicts sent to
New South Wales were moved on to Van Diemen's Land, and
eventually ships from England began to land their convicts
directly at Hobart, the capital of the island. From about 1820,
Van Diemen's Land was receiving a regular flow of convicts
direct from England, and in 1825 the island was proclaimed a
separate colony instead of forming part of New South Wales.
It was the intention of the British Government that the new
colony should remain primarily a penal settlement, a place in
which policy would be determined largely by the needs of the
convict establishement rather than being coloured by the needs
of the free settlers, as had become the case in New South Wales.
However, in the end this proved impossible, and Van Diemen's
Land eventually became a colony of settlement. In 1824 Colonel
George Arthur was appointed Lieutenant-Governor of Van
Diemen's Land, and his methodical administration made transportation a dreaded thing amongst the criminals of London—but
it is convenient to defer discussion of his system until a subsequent chapter.

By the time that the first member of the Solomons family
had been put on board a transport vessel, the establishment of the
penal settlement on Van Diemen's Land had taken place, and it
was in that colony that the family was to be reunited. Ann
Solomons and the four youngest children arrived there first, in
June, 1828. The *Mermaid* sailed from London on 24th February,
but met adverse winds in the Channel and did not clear Land's
End until the 29th. The surgeon who was in charge of the
convicts, James Gilchrist, recorded in his report that many
prisoners complained of catarrh soon after arriving on the ship,
and of rheumatism, 'which I ascribed to the state of the weather
and the dampness between the decks at the time'. However, he
reported, these ailments soon 'yielded to the usual remedies'.
Most of the prisoners suffered from sea-sickness in the early days
of the voyage, and an obstinate form of constipation remained a

troublesome symptom for the first month or six weeks, 'the usual purgatives' giving little help. The *Mermaid* crossed the Equator on 1st April, and because it passed into the southern hemisphere during the southern winter, the passengers seemed to have been spared the worst rigours of a tropical journey—the average temperature was no higher than 53°F. in the month of May. In that month two of Ann's children were ill: Mark, the baby, aged two, was on the sick list for five days with diarrhoea, and the second eldest of the four Solomons children on board the ship, Anne, aged eight, was ill for a fortnight with a fever. The *Mermaid* arrived at Hobart on 27th June, Ann's conduct on the voyage being recorded as 'becoming and Exemplary'. On 5th July the prisoners were landed. The first contingent of the Solomonses had arrived in Van Diemen's Land.

Chapter Six

REUNION AND SEPARATION

Ann Solomons and the four younger children who had sailed with her were soon joined in Van Diemen's Land by the two elder boys, who, as their mother put it, had gone out to Australia 'as gentlemen to settle'. They had gone first to Sydney, the capital of New South Wales, expecting their mother to arrive at that port; it was the original destination of the *Mermaid*. When they learned of its diversion to Hobart, they crossed from the mainland of Australia to Van Diemen's Land to join their mother, bringing with them 'two cartloads of baggage'. Isaac Solomons joined his wife and children shortly afterwards.

Ikey's journey to Australia brings his movements back into the realm of fact after the blank period which follows his escape from Newgate in May, 1827. What happened to Isaac in the year after his escape is not known. He himself declared, in a petition to the Home Secretary, that he left England in the month of his escape and sailed for America—he does not say specifically that he went direct from England to America, but that is the implication of his remarks. However, in one of the accounts of his life he is said to have spent a couple of months in hiding in Highgate, then on the northern outskirts of London, and we know that John Solomons went to Highgate in June, 1827, for the avowed purpose of getting money from his father. Ann, in an affidavit in September, 1827, swore that her husband was 'now of North America, as she believed'. She also spoke of John having visited the United States, and perhaps he had gone to see his father. However, there really was not much time for the journey that John Solomons was supposed to have made—before 19th September Ann said he was 'either in North America or on his return from that country', but we know he was still in London on 30th June—and perhaps the suggestion that he had gone to the United States was part of an elaborate scheme to conceal the fact that Ikey was still in England. There is a story that Ikey went first to Denmark, or at any rate escaped from England on a Danish vessel, before going to New York. One of the accounts of his life says that he was active in forging notes in New York, and another says that he had to leave the United States because a forgery he was engaged on was discovered. Another writer says that Ann's arrest made Ikey 'the subject of much unworthy suspicion even in the Jewish quarter of New York'. On the other hand, as explained in an earlier chapter, an Ikey Solomons of notorious character was active in London in March, 1828, and it is at least possible that this was our Ikey. All this is speculative, but although there is no proof that Ikey went to the United States there is evidence that he crossed the Atlantic to America.

The first certain step in his movements after his escape is that on 10th July, 1828, he left Rio de Janeiro in the ship *Coronet* heading for Van Diemen's Land. He shared a cabin with the Reverend Dr. Browne, a chaplain joining the government service in Van Diemen's Land, who later complained about such a cabin-mate being thrust upon him. Ikey travelled under the name of Isaac Slowman, and the elder boys had used this surname as well. It is not uncommon for families with a foreign-sounding or Jewish-sounding name to change it a little to a more English form, but Ikey may have been trying to conceal his identity. It was certainly dangerous for him to return to British territory, but he had heard of his wife's conviction and was travelling to join her, 'to gain the Society of an affectionate wife', as he himself put it. Whether he was in London, New York or South America when Ann set sail for Australia in February, he would have had time to reach Rio by 10th July, for the journey from England to that port could take less than sixty days. The Chief Police Magistrate of Van Diemen's Land, Josiah Spode, reported to the Colonial Secretary (the head of the administration under the Lieutenant-Governor) that he had heard, before the arrival of the *Coronet*, that Ikey was at Rio, waiting for an opportunity to join his wife. However, this information does not help us to decide whether he was staying in Rio, or whether he was merely en route from England or the United States. But wherever he had been in the period since his escape from Newgate, Isaac Solomons arrived in Van Diemen's Land on 6th October, 1828.

When Ikey arrived he found that most of his family was living in the house of Richard Newman, an officer on the staff of the Chief Police Magistrate. Ann had been assigned to Newman as a convict servant, and she had taken with her the youngest child. The other three children had been placed in an orphanage in Hobart, and John and Moses, the two adult boys, lodged with the Newmans. John Solomons recorded later that 'Mr. Newman did not ill-treat my mother'—the Solomonses lived happily with the Newmans, he said, Mrs. Newman treating Ann more as her sister than as a servant. Indeed, the servant at the house next door said she had never seen Ann do any work, as Mrs. Newman 'does all the Drudgery of the house'. Perhaps the Solomonses paid enough for Ann, too, to be regarded as one of the lodgers. When Ikey arrived in Hobart he also boarded and lodged at the Newmans'. Newman did not report Ikey's arrival to the authorities, and his superior, Josiah Spode, was angry that one of his officers should hide the fact that he was sheltering 'so notorious a criminal'.

The happy relationship between the Newmans and the Solomonses did not last for long. Both John and Isaac Solomons wrote down their side of the story of the quarrel, John in Van Diemen's Land in November, 1828, Ikey in Newgate Prison in London in 1830. Ikey's version was that 'Newman having heard from Report that I was possessed of property' allowed him to stay in his house, 'but I had not been there two days before he applied to me for the Loan of 50 pounds. I lent him 25 pounds and intimated to him my inability to lend him more.' Newman charged Ikey seven pounds ten shillings a week for the five weeks he boarded and lodged with him, 'and in consequence of my inability to lend him the whole sum of fifty pounds his treatment towards my unfortunate Wife was most dreadful—her

Mistress frequently assailed her with the most opprobrious Epithets and ill-usage till I was ultimately compelled to make my complaint to the Magistrates there from whom they received a severe reprimand'. John told substantially the same story, but in his version he himself had lent Newman the money; John's story repeats the suggestion that on being refused the loan of a second £25 Newman drew up a bill for board and lodging which was considered to be exorbitant. Mrs. Newman, he claimed, flew into a rage, and struck Ann and drove her out of the house. Ann claimed that Mrs. Newman 'caused all the trouble', and it may have been a dispute between the two women that led to the breach between the families.

Newman, for his part, declared that Ann's conduct changed after her family's arrival in the colony, and reported that he 'had every reason to believe' that it was her husband's intention to get her away from Van Diemen's Land. (Ikey alleged later that Newman made this suggestion 'from motives of revenge' because of the reprimand which he and his wife had received from the magistrates.) Newman suggested that Ann should be sent to the Female Factory—the depot where women prisoners were held until they were assigned to a settler—although he added for good measure that her husband had already boasted that his influence would be sufficient to get her out of the Factory.

As a result of this quarrel the connection between the Newmans and the Solomonses was severed. Ann's assignment to the Newmans was cancelled, and she was sent to the Factory at Cascades, 'in which place of oblivion', wrote Ikey in December, 1828, 'she is now confined to the utter discomfiture and bereavement of your unhappy Memorialist and his six children'. Isaac or John bought a house and lived in it with the youngest child, while the three other youngsters remained in the King's Orphan School.

There now commenced a struggle to obtain Ann's release from the Factory. John Solomons applied to the authorities for his mother to be assigned to him as a servant, so that they could get the other children out of the orphan school and establish a home. Isaac later went several times with John to the Police

Office to reinforce his request. On one occasion, in great distress, he confessed his identity to the Chief Clerk and said that he must have Ann assigned to him: he would 'brave all for the sake of my dear wife and children'. In December, 1828, Ikey applied to the Lieutenant-Governor in writing asking for his wife to be assigned to him. He said that he was fifty years old, and had travelled 30,000 miles to 'spend the rest of his days in the bosom of his wife and family'. On hearing of his wife's transportation, he had come at once to Van Diemen's Land because of 'those natural causes, feelings and affections unnecessary he trusts here to explain'. A local newspaper commented later that it was, 'let this man be whatever he may, a most redeeming quality to his blackest sins, that such was his affection for his wife and children, that he preferred sharing their fate at the risk of the most serious consequences, to the certainty of securing his own personal safety. . . . These . . . are qualities of some redemption for his offences, be such what they may.' These feelings may have been shared by the Lieutenant-Governor, Colonel George Arthur, but at first he was unresponsive.

Ikey declared that he was willing to enter into a bond of indemnity to remain in Hobart Town at least for the period for which his wife was sentenced to be transported, and to be responsible for her conduct for that time. He had already, he said, taken a leasehold house worth £400 for the family home. The initial reaction of the authorities was wholly unfavourable. Arthur minuted on 19th December that 'the ends of justice would be entirely defeated if his wife, so soon after her transportation to this colony, should be assigned to her husband'. However, the Solomonses kept up the campaign to get Ann assigned to her family. Ikey said later, truthfully or not, that he 'offered to the Governor my services in the capacity of a Convict for the term of four years if he would afterwards allow me to remain there and then be under a sacred pledge, nay, I even offered security to any amount which it was in my power to give that I would not then adopt any means to effect her escape'. When this offer was rejected Ikey found a number of respectable people who were willing to join him in entering into a bond that Ann would remain in the colony. Two of them, Robert Mather, a well-known draper in Hobart Town, and Simon Fraser, another Hobart storekeeper, wrote to the Lieutenant-Governor to explain their reasons for doing this. Mather said that he was 'induced from motives of humanity' to join in signing the bond: he trusted that he would not be regarded 'as an encourager of or an apologist for crime but as acting from seeing her apparently endless confinement and separation from her children, which she is doatingly fond of, and daily witnessing the confusion and unsettled state the family is in (living next to me)'.

The pressure on the authorities was successful: on 16th March, 1829, Arthur minuted 'Mrs. Solomon may now be assigned to her husband.' A bond had been entered into on 12th March, whereby a number of people undertook to forfeit a total of £2,700 if Ann Solomons should 'at any time be clandestinely or unlawfully removed from the said island of Van Diemen's Land' and did not 'until the expiration or remission in due form of law of her said term of fourteen years' transportation remain within the said island'. Isaac Solomons was bound in the sum of £1,000, and John for £500. Robert Mather bound himself in the sum of £200, as did Simon Fraser, John Fawkner who, like Isaac and John, was described merely as a 'gentleman', Benjamin Morris, Joseph Lester, and Richard Pitt, all publicans. The signatures to the bond are shown in the illustration on plate 8.

It might seem that the happy ending had now come to the story of the Solomonses. Isaac and Ann were re-united and, with their children, were living in Hobart Town. They were not short of money—Ikey had been able to buy a house, and had used for part-payment the sum of £300 which Ann had in her possession while in the Factory. The Lieutenant-Governor, when Ikey applied to be allowed to receive Ann's £300, said that it was 'most improper' for a convict to have such a sum of money on her, but he allowed the two to meet so that Ikey could have the cash. As well as the house they lived in, Ikey had bought a general store in Liverpool Street, Hobart Town, where Ann helped him serve the customers. He also owned another house, which he let out, possibly for use as a public house.

The Lieutenant-Governor's willingness to allow Ann to be assigned to her husband might seem to be proof of official complacency towards the couple. But Ikey had made no secret of his identity, and he had been warned that official moves against him had already been taken. Certainly Governor Arthur had no illusions about Ikey; on one occasion, annoyed with someone of similar name, he declared that 'no two worse men were in the Colony than Judah Solomon and Isaac Solomon'. The Lieutenant-Governor had reported Isaac's arrival in Van Diemen's Land to the Secretary of State for the Colonies in London on 17th October, 1828, eleven days after his arrival. The Chief Police Magistrate had heard a rumour that Ikey was seeking to join his wife, and he soon reported that he believed him to have travelled under an assumed name on the *Coronet* and to be living at the Newmans'. Someone had made a statement to him on oath that Newman had admitted that Solomons was in the colony, and a convict working next door to the Newmans had reported to him that she had seen in the yard of the Newmans' house someone whom she thought 'a good deal like' Ikey Solomons, whom she knew.

The Lieutenant-Governor had immediately discussed the matter with the Chief Police Magistrate and the Solicitor-General, but had not found it possible to take any steps against Solomons. There were newspaper reports of his escape, but this was not sufficient. In an opinion dated 17th October, 1828, the Solicitor-General, Alfred Stephen, reported that he was not aware of any grounds for arresting Ikey, 'the mere probability of his using means to effect the escape of his wife, a convict, does not afford such ground. And, with respect to his own alleged escape from custody, when under committal for felony, or to the felony itself . . . there is no evidence attainable at present by which the necessary facts or either of them (except that the individual really is Ikey Solomons) could be established. The newspaper referred to is not evidence and, even if it were, it would not follow that the man had not been many months

ago re-taken, tried and acquitted.' Arthur reported to the Secretary of State that 'I hope, however, that papers may yet be
found containing such particulars of his guilt, as will authorise
his apprehension, which I shall not fail to effect, if this should be
possible.'

When news of Ikey's arrival in Van Diemen's Land was
received in London, steps were taken to provide the Australian
authorities with the powers that they needed. The Home Office
on 6th May sent to the Colonial Office the six warrants of
commitment signed by John Hardwick on 15th May, 1827, on
the basis of which Ikey had been confined in Newgate, together
with a certificate by John Wontner, the Keeper of Newgate, that
he had received the warrants and that Ikey had been confined
in the prison but had escaped from it. They also sent a handbill
issued at the time of Ikey's escape, containing a description. On
the following day, 7th May, these were sent on to Governor
Arthur with the direction that Ikey should be apprehended and
sent back to England to stand his trial. These papers arrived in
the colony on the *Lady of the Lake* on 1st November. However,
all was not to be plain sailing.

There was by this time no possibility of Ikey's denying that
he was in fact the man who had escaped from Newgate. Three
convicts in the colony had sworn that they had actually seen
Ikey on the day of the escape. William Rust declared that he had
met Ikey when they were both confined in the Nightingale
Ward in Newgate in 1827, and that he had, from the Keeper's
office, seen Ikey getting into the hackney coach to drive off to
Westminster to apply for bail. He had since seen Ikey in the colony.
John Hodsoll said that he had been a law clerk in 1827, and had
known Ikey well. He had seen his departure from Westminster
in the hackney coach after bail had been refused. William
Allensby in May, 1827, had been a constable of the parish of St.
James's, Piccadilly, and had been on duty in Palace Yard, Westminster, on the day of Ikey's escape. He had seen Ikey come out
into the Old Palace Yard, and get into the hackney coach.
Allensby had known Ann Solomons in London, too, and he had
seen both Ann and Ikey serving in a shop in Hobart Town.

This sworn testimony had been received by the authorities before John and Isaac had commenced their campaign to get Ann assigned to one or other of them, and, as a result of that campaign, the pair had had to make statements which left no doubt that Isaac was in the colony. Thus there was no difficulty about identification, but none the less the papers sent out by the *Lady of the Lake* proved legally insufficient.

The difficulty that arose was that the documents sent regarding Ikey Solomons did not, according to some legal opinion at any rate, constitute sufficient authority for his arrest. Hardwick's warrants to confine Ikey in Newgate did not, it was thought, go far enough, while Wontner's certificate of his escape had no legal force at all. In consequence, the Colonial Secretary, John Burnett, a magistrate in the colony, himself issued a warrant for Ikey's arrest and return to England. Isaac was arrested, and his wife was returned to the depot where she awaited a fresh assignment. Ikey later painted the scene. 'Here then was a picture of misery which my pen cannot describe—A Father imprisoned in one part of the Town—the Mother in another amongst the most depraved and abandoned characters and our children wandering about the Town and without either Guardian or protector.'

Ikey did not give up, however. The Lieutenant-Governor reported to the Colonial Office on 8th November, 1829, 'A writ of *habeas corpus* has been invoked on his behalf, and, as there appears some little informality in the documents which have been sent out, I conclude we shall have some difficulty in the case, but', he ended confidently, 'I have no doubt it will be overcome.' He declared his intention of sending Ikey back to England on the *Prince Regent*, leaving a few weeks later. This was not the first available opportunity, as the *Ionia* was leaving before the *Prince Regent*. However, the *Ionia* was 'a very small vessel, and even if he could be removed at the moment I should not deem it a desirable opportunity'.

The proceedings on the application for a writ of *habeas corpus* occupied the Supreme Court of the colony on various occasions between 9th November, 1829, and 2nd January, 1830. The Chief Justice, John Lewes Pedder, found it extremely difficult to make up his mind: 'I have never felt so much difficulty in any case in my whole life.' This was responsible for much of the delay, although the illness of the Attorney-General, Algernon Montagu, played its part as well. The case was at one time adjourned from day to day awaiting his recovery; on one occasion the Solicitor-General appeared at a moment's notice in his place, but he seems to have made things worse by reviving points that had been settled and making a few suggestions that he had rapidly to withdraw. Another part of the delay can perhaps be attributed to the lack of law books in the colony: the Attorney-General on one occasion said that he did not have access to many of the authorities that had been mentioned in the case.

Ikey remained in prison during the proceedings. One newspaper had observed on 16th November that he 'is dreadfully cut up, and says he will starve himself to death'. The next issue of this weekly remarked: 'The idea of Mr. Ikey Solomons starving himself was a very good one, and he certainly appeared very faint while Mr. Gellibrand [Ikey's counsel] argued his cause, and His Honour said he might sit down and rest himself. But people seldom die of starvation, except by compulsion, and Solomons lives still.'

Ikey's counsel was Joseph Tice Gellibrand, who had only a few years previously been dismissed from the post of Attorney-General. The substance of his attack on the Colonial Secretary's warrant for the arrest of Ikey was that 'the felony charged, was admitted to have been committed in England, the oath on which the warrant was issued, was taken in England, and therefore Mr. Burnett had no power to issue a warrant for an offence committed where he had no jurisdiction, and even without oath *before him* of the commission of such offence.' The answer of the Crown on this point was that as the magistrate's warrant was in itself valid, it was not open to the Court to go beyond that and seek to establish whether the magistrate had justification for issuing his warrant. Furthermore, it argued that if the Court was to look behind the magistrate's warrant and ask itself what grounds he had on which to issue it, the evidence on which Burnett had acted in this case was sufficient to justify the Court in refusing the writ of *habeas corpus*. There was lengthy legal argument whether the judge had the right to examine the circumstances in which the magistrate had issued his warrant, or whether a warrant which was legal on the face of things had to be accepted without further enquiry. The Chief Justice seems to have made up his mind that he had the power to examine the evidence on which the warrant was issued. He also concluded that the evidence was unsatisfactory in this case and the warrant unjustified because the offences alleged to have been committed had taken place outside the magistrate's jurisdiction and the statements which were offered in proof had not been sworn to in front of the magistrate himself. 'The warrant itself is the strangest I ever saw,' said Pedder. 'It is evidently drawn by some astute person. . . . I am quite certain such a warrant was never seen.'

On these points, therefore, the Chief Justice was prepared to find for the prisoner, but it seemed that there was another possible justification for the warrant. The Secretary of State in England had the right to issue a warrant of arrest, and it was possible that the Colonial Secretary in Van Diemen's Land had the same power. On 21st November the Chief Justice declared his opinion: 'If it is not shewn that the Colonial Secretary has a right as such [and thus not as a magistrate] to commit this man, I shall certainly discharge him. Unless it is shewn to me that the Secretary of State in England can commit an English subject without oath, and that the Colonial Secretary here possesses the same power with the English Secretary of State, I shall discharge this Prisoner!' Gellibrand contended that the Secretary of State's powers of arrest extended only to cases of treason, and not to a felony such as that with which Ikey was charged; in any event, he claimed, the Colonial Secretary had no power of arrest by virtue of that office. The Attorney-General had no observations to make on this particular point—and indeed was rebuked by the Chief Justice for this. Pedder had said on 21st November 'I really hoped and expected, after what I had stated, that I should have been furnished with some little information as to the power of the Secretary of State to commit without oath.' Receiving no reaction to this comment, on 1st December he complained—'I

I

regret extremely that I have received no assistance whatever on the part of the Crown upon the points as to which I have so much wished and required them'. This led to an angry exchange in which the Attorney-General, 'with considerable warmth', protested against such observations; 'I will not allow your Honour here, or any man in Christendom in private life, to dare to make such observations without repelling them.' The Chief Justice reiterated his point—'I have heard no argument whatever in support of the proposition as to the powers of the Secretary of State and of the Colonial Secretary, and I am most anxious to hear something more on this point'—and adjourned the case once again.

Finally, on 2nd January, 1830, the Chief Justice delivered his judgment. He found in favour of Ikey on the law and the facts of the case, and held that the Colonial Secretary's warrant was unlawful. He therefore granted a writ of *habeas corpus*, to take effect two days later. However, he could not ignore the fact that Ikey was an escaped convict, and felt that he had to demand a large sum as bail for his future surrender. A month previously he had indicated the way his mind was moving: 'If . . . I am to take this case as left to the discretion of the Court, perhaps it will be the best course to admit the bail. I cannot but admit it to be a very hard case. I must, of course, require large bail.' 'And that,' interjected Gellibrand, 'of course he would be unable to procure.' 'It really is a very hard case,' repeated Pedder. In the event, the Chief Justice did what he had thought he would have to do—he granted Ikey bail, but only on very difficult conditions. He insisted that Ikey sign a bond himself for £2,000 and find four sureties to sign bonds for £500 each, guaranteeing that he would proceed by the first opportunity to England and stand his trial. Ikey pointed out to the Chief Justice that he was completely unable to produce bail of such a large amount, and asked him to reduce it, but this was refused. Thus Ikey remained in prison, but the warrant on which he had been arrested had been found insufficient to justify his detention.

This uncertain outcome of the legal action presented a problem to the colonial government. The authorities had been prepared

for the case to go against them. On 20th November the Lieutenant-Governor had consulted the Executive Council of the
colony. There were present only Arthur himself, the Colonial
Secretary and one other member, and the facts that this formal
meeting was held, and that Ikey's affair was the only subject
discussed in the hour-long session, testify to the importance of
the case. Arthur formally notified the Council that there was
reason to believe that the writ of *habeas corpus* would be granted
by the Supreme Court. He had therefore asked the Law Officers
(the Attorney-General and the Solicitor-General) for their advice.
Their solution was that Arthur should issue a warrant 'under his
own hand and seal' ordering the Chief Constable of the island
to apprehend Isaac and bring him before the Lieutenant-Governor,
to be dealt with according to law; and that if he was discharged
by the Court on the Colonial Secretary's warrant he should be
arrested on the Lieutenant-Governor's warrant. The Lieutenant-
Governor read the draft warrant to the Council, and obtained
the Council's agreement to the course of action which was
proposed.

Although the writ of *habeas corpus* did not become effective,
the plan was put into operation. Arthur was uncertain of the
effect on public opinion of the decision to send Ikey home after
the legal decision in his favour, and told the Colonial Secretary
to remove him 'with the least possible public notoriety'. On 23rd
January the Lieutenant-Governor reported to the Colonial Office:
'Great legal difficulties have presented themselves. . . . The Court,
after much and protracted consideration, at length ordered that
he should be liberated, upon bail but upon such bail as he has
been unable to obtain. I have deemed it advisable, on the advice
of the Executive Council and of the Law Officers, to issue my
warrant for his removal to England by the *Prince Regent*, which
vessel sails tomorrow morning. That every possible precaution
might be taken to prevent escape, and as the Master of the vessel
will not in any way be responsible, the Chief Constable, Mr.
Capon, proceeds in charge of the prisoner.' Thomas Capon, on
another occasion described by a local newspaper as 'our worthy,
and active Chief Constable, a Colonist of long standing, and

possessing universal esteem', took with him one of his serjeants, Thomas Macadam. The pair were instructed that Ikey was not to be allowed to have any conversation with the crew or the soldiers on board the ship, and that his guards were to be particularly careful if the ship drew near land, and when they came to the English Channel. On 25th January, 1830, at 5 a.m., Ikey was put on board the *Prince Regent*, which at once set sail for England.

Ikey's comment on the proceedings is worth recording: 'where could have been the policy of sending the distance of 18,000 miles after an already exiled and almost heartbroken man whose intention it was never again to return to this Country [he was back in Newgate when he wrote this] tearing him from his Wife and Family . . . it therefore seems to have been the determination of a few prejudiced persons to deprive me of my life.' One motive suggested in London for his being returned to take his trial was that the property held as evidence could not be released until a verdict had been given on the indictments, but this suggestion, like Ikey's, can be dismissed. There need have been no special reason for the authorities in Van Diemen's Land to want to arrest so notorious a person. The law would be put into disrepute if an escaped prisoner, above all a well-known receiver, was not proceeded against.

However reasonable his motives, the Lieutenant-Governor's actions raised the storm that he had foreseen. George Arthur was not popular with all sections of colonial opinion. Gellibrand, Ikey's counsel, had lost his post as Attorney-General because of undue association with an opponent of government; Montagu, his successor in the post, was Arthur's nephew. Since his dismissal Gellibrand had become the editor of an opposition newspaper, which took every opportunity to attack Arthur and his regime. Arthur was in fact engaged in a bitter battle with the press, and was seeking to control the virulent criticisms of his administration which often appeared. Thus Ikey's case was to some extent involved in a political battle of wider significance. One opposition paper, the *Colonial Times*, indeed supported the Lieutenant-Governor's action, saying that justice called for such a step to be taken. This newspaper had been scornful of Ikey's claim throughout. It had admitted 'either that the Home Government had a very exalted opinion of their own power, in controlling in a summary manner, the proceedings of their Colonies, or they consider the institutions of Van Diemen's Land as perfectly insignificant, when placed in the scale against their orders, other-wise in a measure of so much importance to the well-doing of Society, as the bringing to justice of a notorious offender, a loophole would not have been left, for legal ingenuity, opening the door to discussions upon the validity of every part of the proceedings.' However, the paper had suggested that it was merely Solomons's money that made it possible for the legal points to be fought at such great length, commenting on the power of money in 'transforming vice, frightful, hideous vice, into all the natural beauty and comeliness of virtue'. It criticized the Chief Justice for his delay in reaching a decision and for being unduly influenced by Gellibrand's reasoning. Gellibrand's own paper, the *Tasmanian and Australasian Review*, had of course been on Ikey's side. It had praised the Chief Justice for standing up to the pressure which it felt he was under from the Colonial Secretary, the Attorney-General, and the Solicitor-General, as well as the Chief Police Magistrate. After Ikey had been sent home, the paper declared 'that glorious privilege, the right of *habeas corpus*, has turned out to be an unsophisticated humbug' and a little later it wrote that 'Englishmen in the Colonies have no protection whatsoever from the celebrated *habeas corpus*'.

The debate that raged in Van Diemen's Land over the principles raised in the Solomons case was echoed on the mainland of Australia; there too the relationship of the government to the settlers and the Press had given rise to tricky problems, and there too the banner of liberty was being waved. But Ikey was un-aware of what was going on, and of course it could not help him. Thomas Capon had faithfully discharged his duty—the Secretary of State for the Colonies told the Lieutenant-Governor that he had 'every reason to be satisfied with the manner in which Mr. Capon appears to have executed the service entrusted to him'. On 27th June, 1830, Isaac Solomons entered Newgate for the third and last time.

Chapter Seven

THE FINAL TRIALS OF
IKEY SOLOMONS

Isaac Solomons's first action on his return to England was to try to recover some of the property he had left behind him—'my own bona fide property which I had purchased of several respectable Tradesmen in the City of London and which I had Documents to prove'. This property, he insisted, was 'quite distinct' from that forming the subject of the indictments against him. He declared that he had left the property in question 'in the care and for the management and use of my wife and family', and was probably speaking of the goods found in the Henry Street and Bell Lane houses at the time of Ann's two arrests. The property had all been seized and Ikey alleged that the two officers concerned, whom he named as Schilling and Goodwin, 'under the impression that it was my intention never again to return to this Country', turned the property to their own use. 'I can prove that several persons have from time to time purchased small quantities of cloth from such officers.' On Ikey's request the sheriffs of London called the officers before them and enquired about the goods, but they accepted the answer that was given them—that most of the property had been handed over to its owners and that the rest of the cloth was moth-eaten. According to Ikey the officers were unable to produce any accounts, but it would be dangerous to rely on his version alone, and that is all that is available.

In telling his story of unfair treatment by the officers, Ikey had to account for the fact that he could not produce documents to show that the property was honestly acquired by him, although he declared they were available at the time of the seizure of the goods. Some of the documents, he said, were taken with the goods by the two officers, while the remainder 'I deposited with my then Solicitor Mr. James Isaacs prior to my departure for America [a rather casual way of referring, in a petition to the Home Secretary, to his escape from Newgate and flight from England!] for the purpose of transacting any business that might be requisite relative thereto'. Why then had Isaacs not looked after Ikey's interests? Because although 'he knew perfectly well . . . how I became possessed thereof . . . although there are men in the City of London considered respectable and reputable . . . who . . . effect large purchases and realize immense profit under precisely similar circumstances—yet my Solicitor in my absence . . . chose to give way to popular prejudice [and] has from information which I have received acted in collusion with the above named Officers and actually participated in what I may justly term their plunder'. We know that James Isaacs had been accused by Ann in 1827 of converting some of Ikey's property to his own use, and perhaps there was some justification for the Solomonses to complain of their agent's conduct. But criminals who have been brought to book often complain of conspiracies against them by former associates and, as only one side of the story is available, the charges against James Isaacs and the two officers must be regarded as non-proven at best. Ikey certainly did not get any property back—even his application for 'a few pounds for my subsistence while in prison and to enable me to conduct my defence' was refused. However, he had not long to worry about such preliminaries, for the more serious business for which he had been brought back from Van Diemen's Land was soon commenced.

Within a fortnight of his return to Newgate, with what was in the circumstances remarkable speed, Isaac Solomons appeared in the dock at the Old Bailey. Between the 8th and 13th July, 1830, he was tried on eight of the thirteen indictments existing against him. The news spread early on the morning of 8th July that he was to appear that day, and a crowd of people, mostly Jewish, thronged the court. Shortly after nine a.m. Isaac was put in the dock, and the indictments against him were read; 'by

half-past ten o'clock the court became exceedingly crowded, and
the utmost anxiety was manifested for the commencement of
the trial.' However, the rapidity with which the proceedings
had been arranged had been too great: 'owing to some of the
witnesses not having arrived, it was shortly afterwards made
known that the case had been postponed until five o'clock in the
afternoon.'

The first five offences for which Ikey was tried had been committed in the City of London, and these indictments had therefore been laid before the City of London Grand Jury, who had
found them true bills. The cases were heard before the Recorder
of the City and a London jury, the five separate trials taking
place on Thursday, 8th July, and Friday, 9th July, the first and
second days of the sessions. Ikey looked unwell, and was 'indulged
by the court with a chair'—usually prisoners had to stand throughout the proceedings. When the first case began at 5 p.m. on 8th
July, Mr. Clarkson, prosecuting counsel, warned the jury 'not
to suffer the very great notoriety which marked the character
of the prisoner to weigh with them'. This advice was certainly
heeded, for after a few minutes' deliberation and without leaving
the box the jury found Solomons not guilty. He was acquitted
on the second charge the same evening. The next day, starting
again at 5 p.m., the jury went on to acquit him of the other
three charges, in one case by direction of the Recorder because
of the death of the prosecutor and the absence abroad of a vital
witness. On the first day Ikey was defended by Mr. Phillips,
but on the second and subsequent days Mr. Clarkson, who had
prosecuted him on the first day, joined Phillips and both men
acted for the defence. Mr. Curwood took over the task of
prosecuting. (It would of course be impossible today for a
barrister to switch roles so rapidly.) Ikey no longer employed
James Isaacs to act as his solicitor, and 'Mr. Harmer had the
management of the prisoner's defence'.

All the London indictments concerned property which had
been found in Solomons's room in Lower Queen Street in
April, 1827. Although Ikey was known to all and sundry as a
receiver, he was charged with stealing the property. Indeed, three

of the indictments charged him with the more serious crime of burglary—breaking and entering a dwelling house during the night. One of these indictments, for example, charged against 'Isaac Solomons late of London Labourer' that in the night of 5th February, 1827, he did 'burglariously break and enter the dwelling-house of James McKenzie' and stole the following miscellany of goods: '174 table-cloths, value £117; 6 dozens of napkins, value £8; 3 other napkins, value 18 pence; 16 men's hats, value £16; 24 pieces of Irish linen, value £31; 3 pieces of linen sheeting, value £6.17.0; 3 pieces of bed-ticking, value £20.14.0; 1 piece of Holland, value £5.19.0; and 6 pieces of silk handkerchiefs, value £5'. The other burglary charges concerned the property of Groncock and Copestake (some of which Sampson Copestake had managed to have returned to him in 1827, to minimize his losses) and of John Dewis—in both cases a miscellaneous collection of lace, cloth of various kinds, and made-up garments. The two simple breaking-and-entering charges concerned the property of Thomas Neal—the prosecutor who had died by 1830—and John Baker; again the property was cloth, with some shawls as well in the latter case.

The procedure in the five cases was the same: the owners or their servants testified to the loss of the property, identifying the articles produced in court; James Lea identified the property as having been found in Jane Oades's house; and Mrs. Oades said that it was Solomons who had brought it there. In each case the evidence against Ikey was simply that the property which had been stolen could be proved to have been found in his possession. Ikey's reply in each case was to deny that he had any knowledge of or part in the theft, and to declare that he had 'bought the property found in his room at different sales, and in the regular way of business'; he was 'a dealer in a large way' in such articles. Although it was possible that Ikey had acquired the goods honestly, evidence of the possession of stolen property would, in certain circumstances, have been enough to convict him of the theft. As a legal authority of the day put it: 'Wherever the property of one man, which has been taken from him without his knowledge or consent, is found upon another, it is incumbent on that other to prove how he came by it; otherwise the presumption is, that he obtained it feloniously.' If the period between the stealing of the property and the finding of it in the possession of the accused was short enough, the courts would (and still will) presume that he in whose possession the property was found, was the actual thief.

Various cases in the early nineteenth century set limits to the time required to establish a charge of larceny. In Cockin's case (1836) Mr. Justice Coleridge suggested that if a watch were found in a prisoner's possession a month after being stolen the presumption that the prisoner was the thief 'would be greatly weakened, because stolen property usually passes through many hands'. In Partridge's case (1836) Mr. Justice Patterson said that the length of time was to be considered in conjunction with the nature of the article stolen. The period there was two months but, as the goods were unfinished pieces of cloth not likely to be sold in honest trade, the judge allowed the case to go to the jury, and Partridge was convicted. These cases were decided after Solomons's, and at Ikey's trial his counsel cited the then most recent case—Adams's case (1829), in which the period was three months and the property was a saw and other tools. In that case the judge had felt that the duration of time between the theft and the discovery of the goods was too long for there to be any presumption that the prisoner had stolen them. He had therefore instructed the jury to acquit the prisoner without calling on the defence. Two of the indictments against Ikey involved relatively short periods, the property having in one case been stolen in February, 1827, and in another in April of the same year; as the property was found in May, the periods were three months and one month. In another case the period was five months, and Ikey's counsel objected that the proper charge should have been one of receiving stolen goods, but he was over-ruled by the Recorder. In the last two cases the periods involved were longer still, nine months and ten months. Isaac's counsel made even more determined efforts to get the Recorder to rule that the period was too long, but he had no success and the Recorder insisted in each case on letting the facts go to the jury for their decision. However, the jury interrupted both summings-up in their haste to acquit Ikey on these charges.

Ikey was no doubt greatly relieved at having been acquitted on the five London indictments, but he now had to stand his trial on three Middlesex indictments. He had a week-end of rest, for although the courts sat on Saturday, Ikey's case was not called until Monday, 12th July, when he appeared before Mr. Serjeant Arabin and a Middlesex jury. The first trial dealt with the McCabe and Strachan case, the one which had started the downfall of the Solomons family by leading to Ikey's original flight. This had much in common with the London cases, the essence of it being simply that stolen property had been found in Ikey's possession. The goods had been stolen in December, 1825, and had been found in the house in Bell Lane in May, 1826, five months later. Although this period was shorter than that in some of the London cases where Ikey had been charged with the theft, those responsible for the McCabe and Strachan prosecution were more cautious, and merely charged him with receiving the goods. This is why it was a Middlesex case—the property was stolen in the City of London, but as it was found in Ikey's possession in Middlesex the receiving charge was a matter for the county's courts. The indictment alleged that: '14 watch movements of the value of £100 of the Goods and Chattels of Robert McCabe and Charles Strachan by a certain ill-disposed person to the Jurors . . . unknown then lately before feloniously stolen taken and carried away he of the said ill-disposed person feloniously unlawfully and unjustly did receive and have (he the said Isaac Solomons then and there well knowing the said Goods and Chattels to have been feloniously stolen taken and carried away).' Once again the jury were warned by the prosecuting counsel to dismiss from their minds any prejudice against the prisoner. The case was, however, more clear-cut than the earlier ones. The property had been found in Ikey's possession, and rather than attempt any explanation at the time he had fled the scene. Nor had Ikey any defence to offer at the trial—'I leave it totally to my counsel,' he said. He can hardly have been very surprised when he was found guilty (although he later wrote indignantly that the jury was prejudiced). His counsel objected against the indictment on a technical point of law (consideration of which can be deferred for a moment) and sentence was therefore postponed.

Ikey did not have much to worry about on the second Middlesex indictment, which charged him with stealing a watch belonging to one Joseph Armstrong of Liverpool, found in his possession in Lower Queen Street, and the case was soon disposed of. Ikey was acquitted on the direction of the judge, as the prosecutor was abroad. Armstrong had been one of those who had had to spend time waiting in London in case Ikey appeared for trial after his escape in 1827, and his absence now meant that vital evidence was lacking.

The third Middlesex indictment, the last of those on which Ikey was tried, was then called, but his counsel, Clarkson and Phillips, objected to his appearing a third time before the same jury: 'As they had tried him so often, they must feel prejudiced against the prisoner.' The plea lacks some of the force it might at first sight possess, for another jury had only a few days earlier acquitted Ikey on five successive charges. Of course the Middlesex jury which was now being challenged had convicted Ikey on the first charge they heard against him, so one can understand what his counsel had in mind! The judge was reluctant to give in to the plea made to him: he 'did not like to make a precedent. . . . He was sure the jury would do their duty'. However, several of the jurymen said that they did not wish to try the case, and the judge, Mr. Serjeant Arabin, went to consult some of the High Court judges who were in the building. On their advice he agreed to allow the case to stand over until the evening, when another jury could hear it, but after further persuasion agreed to postpone the hearing to the next morning.

Ikey gained nothing by the delay. The indictment charged him with stealing twelve pieces of valentia cloth, valued at £88, the goods of Daniel Deacon. The goods had been stolen some two months before they were found in Lower Queen Street. As this was a stealing charge, Isaac was again vocal in his own defence: 'I never committed a robbery at all; I know nothing of it whatsoever'. The jury retired for half-an-hour's deliberation, and then found Ikey guilty. As the period between the theft and finding the goods in the prisoner's possession was fairly short, the fact that he was convicted was not out of the ordinary. Ikey, perhaps not unnaturally, thought differently. His comment on this episode is worth quoting, even though he is not very accurate about the facts. After having recounted his acquittal in the early cases by 'a merciful Jury', he explains that when the other indictments were tried, 'my Counsel felt it his duty from the great prejudice which existed in the minds of the Jury to challenge the whole of the 12 first impannelled—unfortunately the next 12 were equally prejudiced—for without a tittle of Evidence establishing the fact I was found Guilty upon both Indictments . . . the apparent unanimous disposition of the Jury to find me Guilty was most striking—so much so that it occasioned the following remark from my Counsel Mr. Clarkson—"Guilty! Oh, it is Ikey Solomons he must be Guilty—if Gentlemen it had been the case of any other person the result would have been different" . . . to convict me as an actual Thief must appear to every unprejudiced mind not only cruel but a thing unprecedented.' It is unlikely that Clarkson did make the remark in quite the terms attributed to him, for it is hardly a fair one in view of the earlier acquittals. In addition, it is hardly likely to have come from one who was actually counsel for the prosecution in some of the earlier cases against Ikey. But perhaps the last phrase in the quotation is the key to Ikey's outburst—his professional pride as a receiver was outraged at the suggestion that he was actually engaged in theft himself!

Ikey had thus been convicted on two indictments for felony, but sentence was not passed on him pending the settlement of the legal point which had been raised at the trial of the McCabe and Strachan charge. In Ikey's day our modern system of appeals in criminal cases had not been introduced and the only way in which a prisoner could have his case reviewed by a higher court was to persuade the judge who actually tried him to reserve a point of law for the consideration of all the judges. When this was done, the trial judge would report the circumstances of the case and the legal point which had arisen to the judges in Westminster Hall, who would give a binding ruling, if necessary by a majority vote. This informal procedure was regularized by statute in 1848, when the Court for Crown Cases Reserved was set up. However, it was only with the establishment of the Court of Criminal Appeal in 1907 that a prisoner's right to appeal was fully recognized, and that it became possible to appeal on a question of fact and not merely of law.

The absence of a formal right of appeal did not, however, mean that the interests of the accused were neglected. Judges were quick to prevent any departure from the letter of the law. The judges of earlier times are often represented as being bloodthirsty creatures anxious to hang as many as possible of those who appeared before them. In actual fact, the severity of punishment in earlier times led the judges to lean over backwards in their attempts to be scrupulously fair and to be sure that no one was unjustly convicted. There were, of course, occasional sadists and occasional severe judges (like Mr. Justice Page of Queen Anne's day, who told someone who enquired about his health that he was 'still hanging on . . .'). But most judges were glad to take advantage of opportunities to moderate the harshness of the legal code, and would not allow convictions on charges which carried the death penalty unless the strict letter of the law had been complied with by the prosecution. The slightest slip in any one of the elaborate technicalities of a trial would result in the acquittal of the prisoner. As Parliament declared in the preamble to an act of 1851 which allowed courts to make corrections of minor errors in wording or spelling: 'Offenders frequently escape Conviction on their Trials by reason of the technical Strictness of Criminal Proceedings in Matters not material to the Merits of the Case.' For example, a prisoner was acquitted in 1845 because the name of one of the magistrates who had formerly convicted him was in one document spelt as 'Dalivon' and in another as 'Dalison'—and there was no need to have mentioned his name at all!

Someone who was in Newgate just before Ikey Solomons's last visit there had a lucky escape because of the strictness with

which the law was applied to the prosecution's case. John Puddifoot was tried at the Old Bailey in January, 1830, on a charge of
stealing a sheep, a crime which at that time carried an automatic
sentence of death, although it was very rare for anyone actually
to be executed for the offence. After the summing-up by Mr.
Justice Parke, one of the officials of the court pointed out that
the indictment described the stolen animal as a sheep, but in the
evidence given in court it had been described as an ewe. As the
statute under which the prisoner was charged referred to 'any
ram, ewe, sheep or lamb', it was argued that a sheep and an ewe
could not be considered to be the same thing. The prisoner's
counsel had not spotted the discrepancy but he happily adopted
the argument and objected to a conviction. In accordance with
the usual practice, the judge 'reserved the case for the consideration of the judges'. The jury was asked for its verdict and it
found the prisoner guilty. If the prisoner had been acquitted the
matter would have been at an end; but now Mr. Justice Parke
laid the facts before his brethren. On 19th February, 1830, he
wrote to the Home Secretary, reporting that 'the case was
considered last term and a majority of the judges were of the
opinion that the indictment was not supported by the evidence,
the term sheep, as they thought from the context of the act of
parliament, not being a general term'. In consequence, he asked
that Puddifoot might 'receive his majesty's most gracious pardon'.
'I suppose there is no alternative but to grant a pardon', wrote
a clerk in the Home Office, with a note of irritation that is easy
to understand; below his minute appear the words '23 Feb 1830
Pardon prepared'.

A year or so after John Puddifoot, Isaac Solomons appealed
to the judges on a point of law. It was a complex one. At common
law, the ancient case law of England, receiving stolen goods was
only a misdemeanour. However, Parliament had by statute made
receivers of certain types of goods accessories after the fact to
the original felony, and thus liable to indictment as felons and
to the heavier punishments which felony carried. One such act,
passed in 1770, covered the circumstances of the McCabe and
Strachan charge. However, even when the 1770 act applied,

accessories could only be indicted for felony if the original thief
had been convicted or was 'amenable to justice'. If he was not
available for trial or his identity was not known (as in the case
in point), the receiver could only be charged with a misdemeanour. Parliament in 1822 had endeavoured to deal with the
point, and to ensure that in appropriate cases receiving stolen
goods should be considered a felony whether or not the actual
thief was amenable to justice. Unfortunately, however, the
wording of the 1822 act was not clear enough to overcome the
scruples of the judges. In two earlier cases decided in 1823 and
1824 the judges had ruled against attempts to prosecute receivers
as felons under the provisions of the 1822 act. Although these
cases were not really very close parallels, Phillips, one of Ikey's
counsel, had been able to make enough play with them to cause
Mr. Serjeant Arabin to reserve the case for the consideration of
the judges, although his own feeling was that Ikey could clearly
be convicted of felony. If Ikey had been arrested a month later
the point would not have arisen, for a new act with much clearer
wording had been passed in June, 1827, and no doubts could
exist in the case of indictments issued after that date. However,
Ikey had been indicted in May, 1827, and although the 1827 act
had long been in force by the time his case came to be tried, he
was entitled to be tried by the law as it stood at the time of his
indictment.

The legal manoeuvring did Ikey no good, however, serving
merely to ensure him a year's extra stay in Newgate. When
eventually his case was considered by all the judges, they decided
by a majority of nine to six that the indictment for felony was
good. Even if the decision had been in his favour, Ikey would
not of course have gone free. There was the other conviction
for felony. Moreover, five indictments for receiving the property
mentioned in the London indictments for stealing had been
prepared against him, and these had been found 'true bills' by
the Middlesex Grand Jury. However, these only charged him
with misdemeanours, because of the circumstances in which the
original goods were stolen, and as he had been convicted on two
felony charges they were not proceeded with.

When the judges had decided against him, Ikey had to re-appear at the Old Bailey for sentence. On 12th May, 1831, looking, according to one newspaper, 'exceedingly pale, and . . . much thinner than on the trial', he was sentenced to be transported for fourteen years. This sentence was criticized at the time as being a lenient one, and a writer in *Fraser's Magazine* objected that a hardened criminal like Ikey was receiving a comparatively mild sentence, whilst lesser criminals were being given death sentences or sentenced to life imprisonment. The statute under which Ikey was convicted set a maximum sentence of fourteen years for the receiving charge, but of course he could have received punishment for each of the two offences separately. No time was lost in getting Ikey out the country. On 31st May, 1831, he left Newgate for the last time, and was lodged overnight in the *York* hulk at Gosport. The next day he was placed on board the *William Glen Anderson*, which sailed for Van Diemen's Land on 2nd June.

The *William Glen Anderson* did not arrive at Hobart until 1st November—Ikey was unlucky enough to have to endure an unusually long passage. His ship took 152 days, against the average at the time of 124 days. Ann had been luckier, and her voyage had taken just the average length of time. Experienced sailor though Ikey Solomons was by 1831, five months in a convict transport, much of the time in tropical waters, must have been a terrible experience. Conditions on the convict-ships were notoriously unsatisfactory.

In the early days, the mortality rate on the journey to Australia had been high. The worst experience had been that of the Second Fleet of 1789-90, whose three ships had set out from England with 1,006 prisoners, 267 of whom died before the Fleet arrived in New South Wales. The prisoners on board the largest vessel, the *Neptune*, were kept in heavy irons and were only allowed on deck in small numbers and at long intervals. In this ship and in the *Surprise*, it seems that the prisoners were deliberately kept short of food. The prisoners on the third vessel, the *Scarborough*, were not treated quite so badly from the point of view of food supplies but, as a result of an attempted mutiny,

K

their treatment was harsh in other ways. The more dangerous of the ring-leaders, after a flogging, were stapled to the deck, and all the convicts were kept closely locked up and given insufficient access to light and air. The Reverend Richard Johnson, chaplain of the settlement in New South Wales, described the arrival of the Second Fleet. 'I beheld a sight truly shocking to the feelings of humanity . . . the landing of these people was truly affecting and shocking, great numbers were not able to walk, nor to move hand or foot; such were slung over the ship's side in the same manner as they would sling a cask, a box, or anything of that nature. Upon being brought to the open air, some fainted, some died upon deck, and others in the boat before they reached the shore. When come on shore many were not able to walk, to stand, or to stir themselves in the least, hence some were led by others. Some crept upon their hands and knees, and some were carried upon the backs of others.' An outcry was caused by the condition in which the convicts had arrived in Australia, and two of the officers responsible were tried for murder at the Old Bailey but were acquitted. However, in consequence of the reports, the naval agents who had been in general charge of the convict-ships were replaced by naval surgeons. Their responsibility was to see that the master of the vessel obeyed the terms of the charter and to ensure the welfare of the prisoners. The experiment of introducing surgeons in the role of government representative on the ships was successful, and the mortality rate declined. However, as was so often the case at this period, the new method was not applied systematically and some vessels sailed without either naval agent or naval surgeon. After 1800 bonuses were paid to the master and surgeon according to the number of convicts who arrived in Australia in good health, and this step too had beneficial results. None the less, from time to time convicts suffered severely on board ship, and in 1814 three ships in succession arrived in New South Wales with the majority of their convicts seriously ill.

Shortly after the disasters of 1814 matters were finally placed on a satisfactory footing. The long wars with France were now over, and time and money could be devoted to other purposes.

The post of surgeon-superintendent was introduced. Every convict vessel had a surgeon-superintendent and he soon came to be the leading authority on board, both the master of the ship and the commander of the guard being expected to do what he asked of them. He was responsible for the rations and had to see that each convict received his due share of properly cooked food, at the appointed meal hours, and an ounce of lemon juice daily. He had to inspect the convicts daily, the sick at least twice a day, and was to ensure that the prisoners themselves and their quarters were clean.

Thus by the time Ikey and Ann Solomons travelled on board the convict-ships, conditions were much better than they had been when transportation began. Yet the prison quarters remained dark and gloomy, and were often badly ventilated. In many ships the convicts' quarters were always damp and dank, water seeping through the ship's seams and wetting their bunks and bedding. In very heavy seas the hatches had to be battened down and, if rough weather persisted for some time, the conditions, particularly in the tropics, were extremely bad. Still worse, however, was a tropical calm. The prisoners were too closely packed for movement, the air in the prison quarters was stifling and oppressive, and the pitch from the seams above them often melted and dropped upon them as they lay in bed. The water ration was low and its quality very poor. The food, however, was generally regarded as satisfactory at the least. By the time the Solomonses went to Australia, the issue of clothing to the transports had become fairly adequate, and the prisoners were reasonably equipped both for the cold and for the warm weather they would encounter on their long journey. By their day, too, the practice had grown up of removing the irons from the prisoners fairly soon after the voyage had commenced.

At the end of each voyage the surgeon-superintendents made a report which eventually found its way back to the Home Office. They commented on the health of the convicts on the journey. The surgeon-superintendent under whose care Ikey sailed, Charles Inches, spoke of the 'unusually healthy conditions in which the prisoners continued during the whole of the voyage'.

This he ascribed to the good weather in the first weeks, as a result of which the convicts were 'kept much in the open air on decks' and were 'thus more capable of enduring the vissicitudes of weather' when they got nearer to Australia. Sea-sickness and constipation seem to have been a regular feature on board the vessels, until the prisoners 'became habituated to their new life'. Both Ann's and Ikey's surgeon-superintendents mentioned their efforts to improve conditions below decks. In *Mermaid*, reported Gilchrist, 'the boards of the lower bed spaces were frequently raised during the day for ventilation'; wind-sails were put in the hatches and every other possible device to improve ventilation was tried. Inches gave more detail of the routine in *William Glen Anderson*: 'Immediately after breakfast, they were all ordered on deck, with the exception of a few, who in rotation remained below, to clean the prisons, which was generally done by dry holystoning that portion of the deck, underneath the sleeping berths, and washing and scraping the gangways, or the common portion of the deck, which was found to be, by much, the most effectual method of cleaning. . . . Throughout the day, the prisoners were encouraged to keep on deck, they usually did until sunset, when they were ordered below, mustered, and the prisons secured for the night.' Although *William Glen Anderson* was sailing into the Southern spring, the last part of the journey, from the Cape of Good Hope onwards, was an unpleasant one: 'we experienced much cold, and very stormy weather, the ship taking in board, much water, which, in spite of every precaution, occasionally flooded the prison decks, the prisoners too by this time, were very indifferently clothed, many of them being without shoes.' No doubt the eventual arrival was a relief to all on board, convicts, crew and guard.

Military guards travelled in all the ships, as a precaution against any attempt by the convicts to seize the vessel. There often were rumours of suspected mutinies amongst the prisoners, although Charles Bateson, the expert on the convict ships, doubts if there was anything more than idle bragging on the topic in the 'twenties and 'thirties. The *William Glen Anderson* certainly had its rumour of mutiny and Ikey Solomons distinguished himself in connection with it. In 1837, Lieutenant-Colonel H. Breton of the 4th Regiment, who had travelled in the ship, told a select committee of the House of Commons about the episode: 'There was a plan formed by two desperate characters, and the man who came forward was Ikey Solomons; and the argument he made use of was this, that he had a great deal to lose, and nothing to gain, if they took the ship, and therefore he came forward to tell us.' This action, it may be said, seems to present-day police officers quite consistent with Ikey's status as a high-class professional criminal.

Van Diemen's Land in the Solomonses' time there was very much under the stamp of the personality of Colonel George Arthur, who became Lieutenant-Governor in 1824. Arthur went to the colony after service in the army during the Napoleonic Wars and after administrative experience in the West Indies. His twelve years of rule in Van Diemen's Land was highly thought of by his official superiors, and on his return to England he was knighted and sent as Lieutenant-Governor to Upper Canada. In 1842 he was made a baronet and appointed Governor of Bombay. He had just been nominated for the highest overseas appointment of all, the Governor-Generalship of British India, when ill-health compelled him to retire. He died in 1854.

Arthur's successful career was a result of method and indefatigable energy. W. D. Forsyth, the author of an invaluable study of Arthur's system of convict discipline, describes a surprise visit by Arthur and his aide to the female penitentiary in Van Diemen's Land: 'Dashing up to the gate at a smart canter, their approach was only announced by the thud of the horses' hooves and the rattling of their accoutrements. Throwing the reins to the orderly, the Governor and his aide passed hurriedly through the gate, only recognizing the superintendents by a stern look and a condescending nod. Leading the way himself he examined and pried into everything. The yards, the cells, the wards, the spinning lofts, the washing and cooking departments, the hospital and nursery—all received the closest inspection. Returning to the office he so far unbent as to make a few remarks to the superintendent suggested by the inspection, to give expression to his wishes, to write a short minute in the visitor's book, and then departed as cavalierly as he came.'

Arthur's title was Lieutenant-Governor, because although Van Diemen's Land was in 1825 separated from New South Wales and made a colony in its own right, the Governor of New South Wales was also the Governor of Van Diemen's Land; the Lieutenant-Governor was his subordinate. However, unless the Governor was actually in Van Diemen's Land, the Lieutenant-Governor had full powers. There is no doubt that it was Arthur and Arthur alone who shaped the destinies of the prisoners in Van Diemen's Land. Indeed, all the colonial governors were left with a great deal of discretion, for neither Van Diemen's Land nor New South Wales received full instructions from the Home government on the handling of the convicts until 1842, late in the history of the transportation system. One explanation which has been put forward is that the Home Office was reluctant to give instruction to officers employed by the Colonial Office, while the Colonial Office did not wish to intervene in something which really affected British rather than colonial interests; but the result was that the colonial governments had to make many decisions themselves.

When the Solomonses arrived in Van Diemen's Land they soon had an opportunity of seeing the man who was to play so great a part in their lives, for Arthur invariably inspected the convicts on their arrival. He always made a speech telling them of the penalties and the rewards their conduct could bring. This visit would take place a few days after the arrival of the ship, for the first step was for the Principal Superintendent of Convicts to go on board to receive the surgeon-superintendent's report about the prisoners and to examine the prisoners themselves one by one. Only very limited information about the prisoners was sent out with the ships but, from the surgeon-superintendent and the prisoners themselves, the Principal Superintendent was able to commence a careful record about each one. Ikey Solomons's convict record (set out in full in Appendix II and illustrated on plate 7) starts with a record of his sentence and offence, quotes the Newgate report that he had been transported before and the hulk report, which was merely the erroneous statement that he was a married man with five children. There is then Ikey's own statement: 'This offence receiving stolen goods— transported about twenty years ago for a pocket-book pardoned in three or four years afterwards Moses Joseph was sent to Sydney for the same offence wife and family in this colony married six children.' Thereafter, throughout the remainder of the prisoner's stay in the colony, his conduct was recorded—disciplinary offences and punishments were noted, and the privileges granted to him were set out. It was this record that was the basis of Arthur's system.

When Arthur took office in 1824, there were nearly 6,000 convicts in the colony and just over that number of free inhabitants; over 20,000 convicts were sent out to Van Diemen's Land in the period 1824–1836, and in the latter year the number of free inhabitants was over 25,000. The convicts were divided into various classes, with carefully graded conditions.

The harshest conditions were experienced by the convicts who had committed serious or repeated offences in the colony itself since their arrival and had been sentenced to perform hard labour under strict discipline in the penal settlements, Macquarie Harbour and Port Arthur. The men with the worst records lived and worked in chains. There were in the early 'thirties something like 500 men undergoing secondary punishment (the name given to the sentence to the penal settlements). In Macquarie Harbour prisoners cut huge logs in forests, carried them by main force to the edge of the water and floated them to the shipbuilding yard. This settlement was abandoned in 1832 in favour of Port Arthur, where the convicts were employed in the coal mines. The Lieutenant-Governor described Port Arthur: 'The very worst class of men are worked in chains at the hardest labour of dragging wood, and so forth. Another class are worked out of chains at hard labour, and those who are best conducted are kept at the lightest labour that is required.' He told a select committee of the House of Commons that the narrow neck of land which con- nected Port Arthur to the remainder of the island was 'guarded by a detachment of soldiers under the charge of an officer, with a line of very fierce dogs stationed from shore to shore. The dogs have been so trained that if there is the slightest noise made they immediately give the alarm either by day or night; and so successful has been such a guard that it is not known that more than two prisoners have ever escaped from Port Arthur: one of these was taken and the other was supposed to have perished in the woods.'

Ikey Solomons spent some time at Port Arthur, not as one of men undergoing this severe punishment but as a minor gaol official. This was his regular job in the colony and he was sent to do a spell of duty at Port Arthur as a punishment for 'some commonplace breach of prison discipline'—it was a less pleasant place than Hobart, even for the officials.

There were punishment grades with less severe conditions than those of the men in the penal settlements. Three classes of convicts were kept at hard labour wherever they were needed around the colony. The worst of these men, those 'of the most degraded and incorrigible character', worked in irons and were kept entirely separate from other prisoners. Others were employed in chain-gangs, in slightly less rigorous conditions. The road-gangs did not work in irons but they were under very strict supervision all the time. All these men had to wear special clothing, the much disliked yellow uniforms marked with black arrowheads.

The main body of convicts were to be found in the two categories of 'public works' and 'assigned servants'. Prisoners were placed in one or other of these groups as they arrived and would remain in them, unless they were sentenced to a punishment grade, until they earned their freedom. The term 'public works' was a loose one, covering all the convicts who were retained in the service of the government except those undergoing punishment. Some of the men on public works were labourers on building operations or in stores, others acted as clerks in a variety of government departments. Ikey Solomons, as a gaol official, came into this category. So too did the convicts—often over 300 in number—who were employed as constables and field police to keep their fellow-prisoners in order. Indeed, all the minor tasks of government in the colony were performed by convict labour.

Convicts 'of superior class'—the occasional educated people—were usually kept on public works. They would probably be put in the higher-grade posts. Those employed as clerks were paid a small salary and given an allowance for clothes, but others were issued with rations and with blue or grey clothing. Men of especially good conduct were allowed to sleep in the town, but most of those on public works had to sleep in barracks. They were allowed to work for themselves on Saturdays.

Apart from those in the better situations, the men in government employ were generally worse off than the 'assigned servants', those convicts who were sent to work for a free settler. About half the convict population was in this category. Prisoners assigned to private individuals were not allowed to live away from their master's house, and were not supposed to be paid wages or allowed spare time in which they could work for themselves. They were supposed to have a pass if they were away from their master's land. On the other hand, the master was obliged to provide the convict with a fixed amount of food (meat, flour, sugar and salt) and was allowed to give him tea and tobacco in addition, if he wished. Each convict servant had to be provided with a palliasse stuffed with wool, two blankets and a rug for bedding, two suits of clothing a year, boots, shirts and a cap or hat. The standard of the lodging provided was regulated, and the convict had to be given medicine when he was ill.

The assignment system was something of a gamble for the convict, for a harsh master could bring severe punishment to his servant. Masters were not allowed to flog the convicts themselves, but it was easy to get a magistrate to order such a punishment. It was common to send a note to the magistrate with the man who was to be punished—he would be flogged and sent back. There was a story that one prisoner, guessing the contents of the note that he had been given, asked one of his fellow-servants to carry it for him; the victim of this trick was flogged despite his protests. Another convict, having been assigned to his wife, was sent by her for a flogging as a way of ending an argument.

However, in 1827 Arthur ended the system of unpaid magistrates and divided the island into nine districts, each in the charge of a salaried police magistrate. This resulted in a stricter system of inquiry into complaints made by masters against their servants.

On the whole, the convicts were well treated by their masters, and indeed some people felt that the general level of treatment was so good as to detract from the value of transportation as a punishment. As one observer in Van Diemen's Land wrote: 'It is true that convicts are sent out here as a punishment. But it is equally true that it is not in the interests of the master to make his service a punishment, but rather to make the condition of the convict as comfortable as is consistent with economy. The interest of the master essentially counteracts the object of transportation, for his sole object is to obtain the most work at the least expense.' Assigned servants were usually given the tea and tobacco allowed by the regulations, and even spirits, as an inducement to work well, and many of them were paid in cash or were allowed to work for other people. There is little doubt that many of the assigned servants were, in material terms, better off in Van Diemen's Land than they had been in England. Moreover, in some cases the assigned servant was freed of most of the burdens of convict status. Prisoners with money would pay their master to be allowed to do only the most nominal of duties —Ann Solomons seems to have made such an arrangement with the Newmans, to whom she was assigned on her arrival in Van Diemen's Land. And clearly convicts assigned to a relative, as Ann was later assigned to Isaac, were only convicts outside their own home.

Convicts of good conduct, whether on public works or assigned servants, could hope to obtain eventually a ticket of leave, which freed them from many restrictions. The general rule was that a convict sentenced to transportation for life could obtain a ticket of leave after eight years in the colony; one sentenced to fourteen years after six years; and one sentenced to seven years after four years. Holders of tickets of leave found themselves somewhere to live and a job by which to earn their living. Some ticket-of-leave men were employed by the government in positions of trust, as constables or overseers of road parties or chain-gangs. Better-educated men could obtain appointment as superintendents of estates, or as clerks to bankers, lawyers, or shopkeepers. Some of them were engaged as tutors in private families. Some married free women and some became wealthy men, by this means or by hard work.

The ticket of leave did not free the convict from the super-vision of the police magistrate—Ikey and his family, even after rising to this status, continued to give the police magistrate of New Norfolk much work to do. The convict's description and place of residence were written on the ticket, and he was not allowed to move without the authority of the police magistrate. Ticket-of-leave men had to attend monthly musters held by the police magistrate, who reported on their habits, connections, characters and mode of life. As Arthur wanted all the convicts to attend church on Sunday, all ticket-of-leave men living within two miles of a church had to attend a Sunday muster. The ticket of leave could be forfeited by misconduct. One convict had his ticket of leave suspended for a time for 'being drunk in church during Divine Service and disturbing the congregation', while another lost his ticket altogether for 'embezzling a bottle of yeast entrusted to his care'.

Convicts progressed from the ticket of leave to the next stage, a conditional pardon, again given as a reward for good conduct. Holders of these pardons were free of the restrictions imposed on ticket-of-leave men and the only difference between them and free men was the rule that they must not attempt to leave the colony. However, a conditional pardon could be revoked if the holder misbehaved. The final stage was the expiration of the period of sentence. At the end of the full period a convict was entitled to a certificate of freedom, and once he had received this he was as free as those who had come out to the colony of their own volition.

Isaac Solomons was put into the public works category on his arrival in the colony, being appointed a javelin man, a minor gaol official in the sheriff's department. This relatively favourable situation may have been his reward for giving notice of the mutiny on board the *William Glen Anderson;* it may have been recognition of the fact that he could read and write. Above all, the authorities probably wished to have so notorious a man under their own eye rather than assign him to a free settler. Indeed, it is possible that there was no free settler who wanted to try to find a job for the famous Ikey Solomons! Be that as it may, Ikey became one of the hundred or so convicts engaged in minor clerical and supervisory duties.

Ikey's position was not a high one. The javelin man ranked below the under-turnkey and the clerk, who themselves were both convicts. A further indication of the lowly nature of his duties is that when he was sentenced to be imprisoned for six weeks in the goal in which he was employed, at Richmond, a few miles outside Hobart, it was noted that he was 'at the same time to attend to his duty as Javelin man'. This sentence was passed on him on 19th November, 1832, as a punishment for 'abusive language . . . turbulent and disorderly conduct'. On 5th December, presumably whilst still serving this sentence, he was charged with 'gross misconduct in preferring false and malicious charges against Mr. I. G. McNeilly conveyed in a letter to the Sheriff' and was sentenced to a further month's imprisonment, again while still continuing to do his duty.

In 1832 Ann Solomons was assigned to one of her sons (the record does not show whether it was John or Moses), and Isaac was allowed to live at home as well, so that the family was re-united. Apart from the boys' earnings, they had an income from rents of property amounting to £3 or £4 a week. Surely this is now the happy ending of the Solomonses' story? Alas, it is not.

There was to be no happy ending for the Solomons family. The origin of the trouble that was to come seems to have been Ikey's transfer to Port Arthur. On 18th July, 1834, as a mild punishment, Ikey was sent to perform duty as a javelin man at the penal settlement there. About a year later, some time in June, 1835, he managed to arrange his release from this post. Someone named Judah Solomon, perhaps a relative, had entered into a bond with the government that Ikey would not attempt to escape and, in consequence, Isaac was granted a ticket of leave.

This was rather earlier than usual—on the ordinary rule it would not have been due until 1837. A condition of the ticket was that Ikey lived at least twenty miles from Hobart Town, and he decided to live at New Norfolk, further up the River Derwent from Hobart. (He had bought some property there in 1829, so the place was not completely strange to him.) He rented a house and tried to move the family there. However, while Ikey had been at Port Arthur there had been an unhappy development: Ann had become the mistress of one George Madden, a former convict who had married a free settler and acquired wealth and influence. Someone wrote sarcastically that Madden's 'fashionable character' was not complete until he took a mistress 'on the approved aristocratic principle of crim. con. with his friend's wife'. ('Crim. con.' was the recognized abbreviation for 'criminal conversation', the technical term of the law in nineteenth-century enticement actions.)

In her new situation, Ann did not take kindly to the idea that she should move to New Norfolk; she wanted to live in one of Ikey's houses in Hobart Town, and demanded that he maintain a second home for her there. The pair began to quarrel, and because of their convict status the government files tell much of the story. The convict records of the two principals bear entries which show how the trouble began. Ikey appeared before a magistrate on 3rd July, 1835, charged with 'drunkenness and violent conduct towards his Family at Sundry times during the last ten Days'. The record continues: 'Equal blame existing on the part of Solomon and his family they are admonished that upon the repetition of such conduct both Solomon and his Wife will be punished.' On Ann's record there appears: 'July 20th, 1835. . . . Disorderly conduct in using opprobrious epithets to her Husband and otherwise Ill-treating him, Disturbances having continued in the Family ever since the Warning given them on 3rd July and appearing to arise from a combination between the Mother and Children against the Father Ann Solomon is returned to the Factory.'

As the record notes, the children took their mother's side in the family quarrel. The two elder sons had left the colony by this time, but David, now aged about seventeen, and Anne, a couple of years younger, had turned against their father. Isaac complained to the magistrates that his wife abused him, and that his son David had assaulted him on 16th July—not for the first time, for he said that the boy had frequently struck him—and had shut him out of the house. Ikey asked for David to be bound over to keep the peace towards him. Witnesses testified to the son's assault on his father and denied the suggestion that Ikey was drunk at the time. Young Anne wrote to the Chief Police Magistrate in August, pleading for the release of her mother from the Factory. She complained that she had to look after the two youngest children in a cottage in Hobart Town, after Ikey had turned them out destitute. She said that it had been her father's intention all along to put her mother into the Factory. She spoke of the 'violent treatment my mother has received from Father since the first day of his return from Port Arthur'.

John G. W. Wilson, a young man who had lodged in the Solomonses' house, wrote to the Police Magistrate of New Norfolk, taking up the cudgels on behalf of Ann. Ikey, he said, had achieved his aim 'of securing from his family the little property on which they were dependent'. Ikey had left his family destitute and had 'turned his daughter out of the house into the open streets, destitute in every sense of the word'. A constable, he said, had merely looked on while this happened, because Ikey had previously 'prejudiced the whole community against her and her family and most effectually secured the District and other constables on his side, a measure which it is well known he had always recourse to both here and in England, consequently he has always plenty of witnesses ready to come forward and swear anything on his behalf that he puts in their mouths, whilst she has not even a friend to speak in her behalf'.

It seems that Ikey was not responsible for the quarrel with Ann, even though the children were not on his side. Thomas Mason, the police magistrate of the district, had formed this view, as the note on Ann's record testifies; he sent her back to custody in the depot. He did not fix the length of time that she was to stay in the Factory, but he believed that 'a little retirement would be

v. beneficial to her character'. Mason did not believe that there was any truth in the charges of drunkenness against Ikey, and indeed when asked to comment on Anne's letter about her father's conduct he said that her complaints were unjustified. Far from turning his family out of the house, Ikey had begged them to stay, 'and is so unhappy at their absence that he has repeatedly applied to me to assist him in recovering them'. He pointed out that Ikey, having rented a house at New Norfolk and being willing to keep his family there, could hardly be expected to maintain a second establishment in Hobart. Mason was equally scornful of young Wilson's letter—Wilson had admitted being in love with Anne Solomons, whom he was later to marry, and Mason called his missive the 'effusion of this love-sick swain'. He repeated that Ikey had begged Ann to remain with him.

Ann was released from the depot on 8th September, 1835, and somewhat surprisingly was granted a ticket of leave on 5th November. She had qualified by time, having been in the Colony seven years rather than the six that was usually demanded before someone sentenced to fourteen years' transportation received a ticket of leave; but she had hardly qualified by good conduct, which was supposed to be equally necessary. Perhaps it was felt that the difference between being assigned to her family and being on ticket of leave was not great. One magistrate later expressed his regret that the Solomonses had been given their tickets, although he apparently did not commence the official procedure which could have led to the tickets being withdrawn.

It is possible that Ann and Isaac continued to live together for some years, for they both received a conditional pardon on the same day, 27th May, 1840. Two years before that Isaac had been allowed to return to Hobart; he opened a shop there and spent the rest of his life in the town. When Isaac and Ann received their conditional pardons, they became virtually free, save only that they were not allowed to leave the colony. Ann would have been free even of this condition in 1841, when she had served her sentence in full, and Ikey in 1844. It seems probable that Isaac and Ann had finally separated by that time, and the three elder boys had left Van Diemen's Land for the mainland of Australia. Anne had married Wilson, her 'love-sick swain', on 4th May, 1840. (Her parents received their conditional pardons three weeks later—perhaps the authorities thought the couple might have a chance of settling down together in the new circumstances, or perhaps it is just a coincidence.) Isaac's younger daughter, Sarah, seems to have remained loyal to him in the family quarrel, and she lived with him until she married Godfrey Barnett Levy on 27th January, 1847.

Isaac Solomons may not have been the easiest of men to live with. Apart from the minor breaches of convict discipline noted earlier, with their references to 'abusive language' and 'disorderly conduct', he had also appeared before the magistrates for 'making use of obscene language to Reuben Joseph in the presence of many respectable females'. This was on 18th February, 1836; 'having expressed contrition and apologized to Reuben Joseph' he was let off with a severe reprimand. Whatever his faults, however, he seems to have been very badly treated by his wife, bearing in mind what he had suffered as a result of going to Van Diemen's Land to join her. He had written of her when he was in Newgate in 1830 that she was 'an innocent woman . . . esteemed by all who knew her as having always walked in a respectable sphere of life—her reputation unimpeached and her virtue unsullied—if I had been Guilty of any crime would I not have suffered even death rather than the consequences of my guilt should have devolved upon the head of an innocent, artless and unoffending wife?' He is unlikely to have written in those terms in later years!

Isaac Solomons died early in September, 1850, being buried on the 3rd of that month. He was then probably sixty five years of age. Although there had been repeated suggestions in England that he had made his fortune in the colony, he seems to have died a poor man: when letters of administration for the estate were issued to his wife, it was noted that the value did not exceed £70.

Thus ended the life of Ikey Solomons. His last few years seem to have been calm, in comparison with the tempestuous times that had preceded them, but one suspects that he must have looked back longingly on his former days in London, when he had been 'the great Ikey Solomons'.

One last point remains to be considered: did Charles Dickens base Fagin in *Oliver Twist* on Ikey Solomons? Some writers have had no doubt that this was so. Thus Professor Philip Collins in his *Dickens and Crime*, remarks that 'Fagin was, as everyone saw, based on the famous Jewish fence, Ikey Solomons'. Professor L. Lane refers to Ikey as the 'real-life model for Fagin', giving the credit for pointing out the connection to E. W. Pugh, who in 1913 wrote, 'Fagin was, I think, founded on the personality of a famous rogue named Ikey Solomons'. However, others have rejected the connection between the two men. M. J. Landa wrote that Fagin 'had no living model, although he is generally supposed to be based on Ikey Solomons, a receiver of stolen goods'. There was, he concluded, 'nothing whatever in the known facts concerning Solomons to stamp him as the model of Fagin'. Harry Stone regards Lane's remark as going 'beyond the evidence', adding that 'Solomons's traits and practices as reported in *The Times* bear no resemblance to Fagin.'

Examination of the evidence would seem to lead inescapably to the conclusion that Dickens did *not* model Fagin on Ikey Solomons. There is first the internal evidence of *Oliver Twist* itself. Although too much weight cannot be attached to the point, there were differences of appearance between the two. Fagin is described as 'a very old shrivelled Jew, whose villanous-looking and repulsive face was obscured by a quantity of matted red hair', whereas the brown-haired Solomons was not active in London after the age of about forty-two. Solomons does not seem to have had the dirty or the miserly habits ascribed to Fagin. The text of the book and Cruikshank's drawings for it always emphasize Fagin's Jewish appearance, but Ikey was able to pass under the name of Jones or Slowman. Furthermore, there is the fact that the stories of the two men do not correspond at any point. Some writers have already called attention to this fact; the fuller information about Ikey's life contained in this book makes the argument even more weighty. Moreover, if Dickens was indeed thinking of Solomons when he created Fagin, one

L

can only say that he did not make very much of his opportunities. Most of the episodes in Ikey's colourful life which have been described in this book were not matters of general knowledge at the time, and some of them might have been difficult to work into the story. But would Dickens have neglected the opportunities presented by a criminal wife? Would we not have had a Mrs. Fagin to place alongside Mrs. Bumble and Mrs. Squeers in the gallery of Dickensian villainesses?

Equally, the external evidence does not lend support to the suggestion that Ikey and Fagin are connected. Landa pointed out that Dickens himself did not mention the alleged connection at a time when he would almost certainly have done so if it had existed. Dickens was greatly upset to find that his creation of the character of Fagin had exposed him to the charge of anti-semitism. He wrote to a Jewess of his acquaintance, Mrs. Eliza Davis, rejecting the charge. He pointed out that 'it unfortunately was true of the time to which that story refers, that that class of criminal almost invariably *was* a Jew'. If he had based the story of Fagin on Ikey Solomons, if he had even remembered the case of Ikey Solomons at the time he was writing to Mrs. Davis, would he not have mentioned him? Would it not have been the strongest possible argument that he could put forward, if he could say that Fagin was not entirely the creation of his own imagination but an adaptation of an existing and notorious Jewish receiver?

A study of the very full biography of Charles Dickens written by John Forster, his friend and confidant, provides further grounds for thinking that there was no connection between Fagin and Solomons. Forster does not mention Ikey. He tells of receiving from Dickens a note saying, 'Don't, don't let us ride till tomorrow, not having yet disposed of the Jew, who is such an out and outer that I don't know what to make of him'—and to this he adds the comment, 'No small difficulty to an inventor, where the creatures of his invention are found to be as real as himself.' There is no hint here that there was a real Jew who could have provided a suggestion as to the fate of Fagin. Elsewhere in the book Forster discusses the extent to which an author draws on real persons when inventing his characters and does not mention Fagin in this connection. Moreover, he refers to 'the only [instance] known to me where a character in one of his books intended to be odious was copied wholly from a living original . . . he had himself a satisfaction in always admitting the identity of Mr. Fang in *Oliver Twist* with Mr. Laing of Hatton Garden.' (Laing was a magistrate of hasty temper and a considerable disregard for the law, who rode roughshod over objections to his arbitrary actions and general rudeness until Dickens's caricature of him led to official action against him.) John Forster was indignant at a story which had been circulated by George Cruikshank, who had drawn the illustrations for *Oliver Twist*, that the original inspiration had been his and not Dickens's. According to this story, Dickens had seen a set of drawings that Cruikshank had made and had woven a story round them, inspired by the evil expression in the face of the character who afterwards became Fagin. Forster refutes this story, and indeed it is doubtful if anybody ever took it seriously. But, again, if Forster had been able to reinforce his argument by showing another source of inspiration for even part of the character of Fagin, would he not have done so?

None of those who have sought to make the connection between Ikey Solomons and Fagin have brought forward any positive evidence in support of it. Landa surmised that the origin of the suggestion was to be found in the fact that the playbill for the Royal Surrey Theatre's production of a dramatic version of *Oliver Twist* in 1838, when stressing that the picture presented by the book and the play was a true one, referred to Ikey Solomons. It is true that the playbill does make reference to Solomons, but it does not in any way suggest that Fagin was based on his life. Landa points out that a play entitled *Van Diemen's Land*, which was staged in London in 1830, had a character named Ikey Solomons, a small part written in to catch the benefit of the publicity attracted by the name. Landa feels that Dickens, when he wrote *Oliver Twist* in 1837–8, may have been reminded of Ikey by this play. This is possible, and it is equally possible that Dickens had read one of the biographies of Ikey quoted earlier in this book. But there was no real need for any direct connection. The novelist Arthur Morrison, writing in 1896, thought Ikey well enough known and well enough remembered to refer to him as the 'Prince of Fences'. W. M. Thackeray thought Ikey well enough known to use the penname 'Ikey Solomons Junior' when he wrote a story in 1839–40 in *Fraser's Magazine*, 'to counteract the injurious influence of some popular fictions of that day'. In just the same way Dickens could well have remembered Ikey Solomons when he was writing *Oliver Twist*. He *could* have remembered him; but there is no evidence that he did, and some evidence, even if only of a negative kind, that he did not remember Solomons, or rather that he did not use him as a basis for his fertile imagination. We shall never know with certainty, but it does not seem that there is any foundation for the claim that Dickens based Fagin on Ikey Solomons. It would have been a fitting end to his story if he had been immortalized by the great novelist. But even without that, Isaac Solomons had a full and varied life.

Appendix I

Ann Solomons's convict record in Van Diemen's Land

129 Solomons Ann
Mermaid June 1828
Old Bailey 13th September 1827—14

Transported for Receiving Stolen Goods Gaol Report: A Notorious Receiver of Stolen Goods—married & 6 children. Stated, this Offence Receiving stolen goods a Watch prosecutor a Captain or Master of a Vessel lived in the Commercial Road—1 girl 7 one girl 5 one boy 9 one boy 3 years old—my husband I believe has gone to America—I have two sons gone to Sydney—John 21 & Moses 18 as Gentleman to settle—my Father is a Coachmaster lives in Aldgate Moses Julian— my husband was a Jeweller—lived in Bell Lane—Married—Jewess.

July 20th 1835 'Ux Isaac Solomon'—disorderly conduct in using opprobrious epithets to her Husband and otherwise Ill-treating him, Disturbances having continued in the Family ever since the Warning given them on the 3rd July and appearing to arise from a combination between the Mother & the Children against the Father Ann Solomon is returned to the Factory for the disposal of the Principal Superintendent—T Mason—

Conditional pardon No. 2396 27th May 1840

Appendix II

Isaac Solomons's convict record in Van Diemen's Land

1407 Solomon Isaac
William Glen Anderson Nov. 1 1831
Middlesex 8 July 1830—14

Transported for Receiving Stolen Goods Gaol Report
Before Transported Hulk Report 'Married 5 Children'
Stated This Offence Receiving Stolen Goods—
Transported about 20 years ago for a Pocket Book
Pardoned in 3 or 4 years afterwards Moses
Joseph was sent to Sydney for the Same Offence
'Wife & Family in this Colony Married 6 Children'—

November 19th 1832 Javelin Man—Abusive language to Mr. Buscombe
& turbulent & disorderly Conduct on the 3rd instant to be imprisoned
in the Gaol at Richmond 6 weeks at the same time to attend to his duty
as Javelin Man—WTP & IHB—*December 5th 1832* Javelin Man—
Gross misconduct in preferring false & malicious Charges against Mr.
I.G. McNeilly conveyed in a Letter to the Sheriff to be imprisoned in
Richmond Gaol One month but at the same time to do the duty of
Javelin Man—IHB & WTP—*July 3rd 1835* TL—drunkenness and
violent conduct towards his Family at Sundry times during the last
10 Days—equal blame existing on the part of Solomon and his
family they are admonished that upon a repetition of such conduct
both Solomon and his Wife will be punished—T Mason—February
18th 1836 TL—Making use of obscene language to Reuben Joseph in
the presence of many respectable females, having expressed contrition
& apologised to Reuben Joseph he is severely reprimanded—AG—

Conditional Pardon No. 2397 27th May 1840
Free Certificate Number 705 1844

10.4.34 PS office 18.7.34 Port Arthur Office 5.7.35 E A Office

Appendix III (a)

Petition from Ann Solomons

To the King's Most Excellent Majesty the petition of Ann Solomon late of Bell Lane Spitalfields, now a prisoner in the Gaol of Newgate and under a Sentence of Transportation for the term of Fourteen years; having been convicted at the last September Sessions held at the Justice Hall in the Old Bailey of having in her possession, a certain Watch, the property of Joseph Ridley; knowing the same to have been stolen;

Most humbly showeth, that your petitioner is deeply impressed with shame and sorrow under her present most distressing, painful and unfortunate situation; and is led earnestly to implore for an extention of mercy, as far as is hereafter humbly submitted to humane consideration.

That your petitioner most truly states, she is a poor, weak Woman, led astray from the paths of rectitude by others. That at the moment she was making speedy preparations for quitting for ever her Native Country, she was led by a certain party, to receive the beforementioned watch into her possession; the duty of which party ought rather to have advised her against such a measure, and not have led her into her present heavy troubles and misfortunes, which at last they were only enabled to do by their most pressing and long solicitations, and which in the end unfortunately proved too powerful for the weakness of her nature to withstand. But who was this party? Her brother-in-law Benjamin Solomon, who had previously laid this plan for entrapping your unfortunate and distracted Petitioner, for the purpose, or as a means thereby, of procuring his father Henry Solomon's liberty; and who has in consequence had a mitigated sentence of six months imprisonment.

That your petitioner has no less than six children viz 4 sons and 2 daughters, part of whom are very young, and one of them still at the breast—. That her children having become destitute of a father in this country, and her property having been all lost, squandered or stolen away, during her troubles, induce your humble petitioner most earnestly to beg and pray, that on consideration of her case, and her own painful situation, together with the forlorn and unprotected state of her children, she may be mercifully granted permission to transport herself out of Your Majesty's dominions, for the full period of her sentence, taking with her the whole of her children, her friends paying the expenses, and furnishing good and sufficient security to that effect. And as in most sincere gratitude and humble duty your petitioner, a miserable woman—a distracted mother, will ever be bound to pray, etc., etc.

Endorsed on Ann Solomon's petition Ann Solomon 34 Old Bailey September Sessions 1827 Receiving stolen goods 14 years transportation Gaoler's report A notorious receiver of stolen goods

Nil January 8th 1828

Appendix III (b)

Petition of Joseph Ridley

To the King's Most Excellent Majesty the Petition of Joseph Ridley prosecutor of Ann Solomon most humbly showeth that your petitioner prosecuted Ann Solomon at the Old Bailey Sessions last September for having in her possession property which your petitioner had been robbed of.

That your petitioner having heard numerous reports in favour of Ann Solomons since her conviction, felt it his duty to use every means in his power to ascertain the truth thereof, and after the most minute investigation from quarters very respectable, your petitioner has learned that the unfortunate woman has been altogether the victim of a bad connection, having been basely tempted and betrayed, by those who ought to have protected her.

That your petitioner since this discovery feels deeply interested in her favour, and humbly hopes that Your Majesty may be most graciously pleased to grant her the prayer of her annexed petition and etc., etc.

Appendix III (c)

Second petition of Joseph Ridley

To the King's Most Excellent Majesty

the petition of Joseph Ridley prosecutor of Ann Solomon most humbly showeth that your petitioner petitioned Your Most Gracious Majesty on behalf of Ann Solomon about eight days since but has not received any reply.

That your petitioner humbly begs leave to represent to Your Most Gracious Majesty that he has again made every enquiry into this poor woman's case and finds she was completely trepanned into her present distressing condition by her brother-in-law in order to exonerate his father who was confined at the time under suspicious circumstances.

That your petitioner has every reason to believe that the watch found in the possession of Ann Solomon was the only article bought since her husband left the country, and that she would not have purchased the same had she not been overpersuaded by her brother-in-law for the beforementioned reason.

That your petitioner after this strict investigation into the unfortunate woman's conduct which he finds very favourable, humbly hopes that Your Majesty will be most graciously pleased to allow her to transport herself with her six children from this country.

That your petitioner having been informed that Your Most Gracious Majesty has been pleased to extend your goodness to several persons similarly situated, and allow them the indulgence of transporting themselves beyond the seas, your petitioner humbly hopes that Your Majesty will be pleased to take the case of Ann Solomon into Your Majesty's most gracious consideration (under all its circumstances it being her first offence) and grant the prayer of her petition etc., etc.

(Public Record Office, H.O. 17/107)

Appendix IV

Bond entered into by Isaac Solomons
and others regarding Ann Solomons

Know All Men by these Presents that We Isaac Solomon and John Solomon both of Hobart Town in the Island of Van Diemen's Land Gentlemen Robert Mather and Simon Fraser of the same place Storekeepers John Fawkner of the same place Gentleman Benjamin Morris and Joseph Lester of the same place Publicans and Richard Pitt of Compton Ferry in the said Island Publican are and each of us is jointly and severally held and firmly bound to our Sovereign Lord the King in the following Penal Sums that is to say the said Isaac Solomon in the Sum of One thousand Pounds the said John Solomon in the Sum of Five hundred pounds and the said Robert Mather, Simon Fraser, John Fawkner, Benjamin Morris, Joseph Lester and Richard Pitt in the sum of Two hundred pounds each of lawful money of Great Britain respectively to be paid to the said Lord the King or his certain Attorney Heirs Successors Executors Administrators and Assigns for which said payments to be made we do bind ourselves and each of us himself jointly and severally and our respective Heirs Executors and Administrators firmly by these presents sealed with our seals. Dated the Twelfth day of March One thousand eight hundred and twenty nine—

Whereas Ann Solomon the wife of the above bounden Isaac Solomon hath been in England convicted of Felony and sentenced to Transportation for Fourteen years under which sentence of transportation the said Ann Solomon is now a prisoner in the *Female House of Correction* in this Island *and Whereas* the said Isaac Solomon has solicited His Excellency the Lieutenant Governor that the said Ann Solomon may on account of her family of children be permitted to leave the said House of Correction with which solicitation His Excellency hath been pleased to comply upon the said Isaac Solomon, John Solomon, Robert Mather, Simon Fraser, John Fawkner, Benjamin Morris, Joseph Lester and Richard Pitt entering into the present obligation, Now the condition of this obligation is that if the said Ann Solomon shall not be at any time be clandestinely or unlawfully removed from the said Island of Van Diemen's Land but do and shall until the expiration or remission in due form of law of her said term of fourteen years transportation remain within the said Island then this obligation shall be void But otherwise it is to remain in full force.

(Signed and sealed by the eight men named)

Signed Sealed and delivered by the above named Isaac Solomon, John Solomon, Robert Mather, Simon Fraser, John Fawkner, Benjamin Morris and Joseph Lester in the presence of J.H. Thompson Clerk to Alfred Stephen Esquire.

(Archives Office of Tasmania)

Appendix V

My Lord, in presuming to address myself to your Lordship's notice I am induced to take that Liberty under circumstances singularly vexatious but, being sensible of the high character your Lordship bears as a public Man and the independent principles invariably manifested by you and the esteem and admiration with which your private character is so justly appreciated and while the tongue of malice has been loud against the unfortunate you have lent a willing ear to their cause and spent your valuable time in deliberation for their good I as an humble Individual have presumed to lay a statement of my case before you in a few of its bearings as it would be impossible for me from my agitated state of mind to enter into a detail of all the circumstances connected with it in the hope that you will after perusing it consider that in taking such a liberty the aggravating circumstances connected with it will warrant my adopting this course.

To enter into a detail of the extreme hardship which I have suffered would be intruding at too great a length upon your Lordship's valuable time I shall therefore content myself by taking a short view of the circumstances connected therewith.

I left England in the month of May 1827 to prevent the dreadful consequences of a feeling which then prevailed against me and with the view of avoiding the consequences which would have been entailed upon my Family by the loss of a Father it being my impression that they intended to take my life—I consequently sailed for America and endured the fatigues of a voyage of many thousands of Miles— shortly after my arrival I was informed that my wife an innocent Woman and helpless Family having been plunged into despair through the malicious artifices and designs of my own Relations—this was effected under the following circumstances—while in America I wrote to my Wife requesting her to purchase a few watches and send them to me as I had been in the habit of dealing in that line for many years she accordingly intimated my wishes to amongst other persons two of my own relations who took advantage of that intimation and hence arose an opportunity of putting their base designs into effect—In compliance with my request she purchased a few of the Articles above named and amongst them was one which proved her destruction—for such I consider it—upon this an information was laid against her as a Receiver of stolen property—I repeat that her own relations were the instigation of this infamous scheme—she was accordingly tried and convicted and sentenced to transportation for 14 years—upon hearing of which I immediately proceeded to Hobart Town where I found her in the Service of a person named Newman with my youngest Child—I ascertained that three of my Children were placed in the Orphan School established there and my other two Sons were wandering about the Town without employment—With the remainder of my once ample but then scanty means I purchased two houses and appropriated one of them to the use of my Family and the other I rented out for their support—Newman having heard from Report that I was possessed of property allowed me to remain with my Wife in his house for the space of 5 Weeks but I had not been there two days before he applied to me for the Loan of 50 pounds I lent him 25 pounds and intimated to him my inability to lend more—I was then convinced that it was not from disinterested principles of humanity that he allowed me this indulgence for during the 5 weeks I boarded and lodged with my Wife he charged me £7-10/- per week and in consequence of my inability to lend him the whole sum of 50 pounds his treatment towards my unfortunate Wife was most dreadful—her Mistress frequently assailed her with the most opprobrious Epithets and ill usage till I was ultimately compelled to make my complaint to the Magistrates there from whom they received a severe reprimand— from motives of revenge Newman then wrote to the Governor of the Colony stating that I wished to get my Wife out of his Service with the intention of taking her and my 6 Children from the Colony—a thing almost impossible—the Governor giving ear to his villainous assertions for her better Security then placed her in the Gaol for the term of 7 months and left me with three of my Children without the assistance of their Mother—after many fruitless applications to the Governor I prevailed on him to release her but not until I produced Security to the amount of £2,700 given by six of the most respectable Inhabitants of the Colony—Shortly afterwards I found that a Warrant had arrived for my apprehension—I was in consequence placed in a prison and my heartbroken wife in a place there called the Factory where her hair was literally shorn from off her head and her treatment in every other respect was the most cruel—without common necessaries—here she was classed amongst the most depraved women without being allowed even the indulgence which was shown to them—here then was a picture of misery which my pen cannot describe—a Father imprisoned in one part of the Town—the Mother in another amongst the most depraved and abandoned characters and our Children wandering about the Town without either Guardian or protector—these are but few of the sufferings which my unfortunate wife has had to contend with—an innocent women who had never till that occasion been before a Magistrate or been the Inmate of any prison but was esteemed by all who knew her as having always walked in a respectable sphere of life—her reputation unimpeached and her virtue unsullied—if I had been Guilty of any crime would I not have suffered even death rather than the consequences of my guilt should have devolved upon the head of an innocent, artless, and unoffending wife?—is it natural to suppose that I should ever for a moment suspect that my wife would have been made the victim of the prejudice which existed against me? such an idea never occurred to me —but alas! it has so happened.

The innumerable other troubles and sufferings which my unfortunate Wife has endured since her banishment from her native Country I can no longer dwell upon from the agitated state of my mind but which if I were here to enumerate would be sufficient to excite the sympathy of a heart of Stone but before I conclude I will take the liberty of stating briefly the misfortunes and losses which I have suffered.—

In the month of May 1827 on leaving this Country I left property behind me to the value of £3,000 in the care and for the management and use of my wife and family—Although this was my own bona fide property which I had purchased of several respectable Tradesmen in the City of London and which I had Documents to prove—the whole of this property together with such Documents was seized and taken to the houses of the Officers who seized it of the names of Schilling and Goodwin who acting under the impression that it was my intention never again to return to this Country have as I have been informed and which I can prove to be true appropriated part thereof to their own use and converted other part thereof into Money—I have recently made application to the Sheriffs for the restoration of my property whose disposition to assist me as far as consistent was most exemplary —they sent for the two officers above named and interrogated them as to the disposal of my property—their answers were that they had made over the greater part of it to several persons who were the Owners and the remainder consisting of Cloth was moth-eaten and could not be produced—Now this fact is worthy of remark that these Officers have not rendered either to the Sheriffs or myself any account as to the disposal of my property but the only satisfaction I can obtain is that they have done this and that but no definitive answer—here then is one of the many injuries which I have suffered—I can prove that several persons have from time to time purchased small quantities of cloth from such officers—The remainder of the Documents relating to such property I deposited with my then Solicitor Mr. James Isaacs prior to my departure for America for the purpose of transacting any business that might be requisite relative thereto—As my legal adviser I made him my Confidant he was fully acquainted with the whole of my affairs—he knew perfectly well where my property was deposited and how I became possessed thereof—Although he well knew and although the world also knew that to denominate me a Thief was as absurd as it was unjust—Although there are men in the City of London considered respectable and reputable under the garb of privileged men who by virtue of their freedom effect large purchases and realize immense profit under precisely similar circumstances—Yet my Solicitor in my absence instead of protecting my property rather chose to give way to popular prejudice which often arises from an unclear knowledge of such circumstances as generally attach to the case of the Victim of their prejudice—he solely with the view of suiting his own purposes has from information which I have received acted in collusion with the above named Officers and actually partici- pated in what I may justly term their plunder—well knowing that I was 18,000 miles distant from my native Country and acting under the impression that it was my intention never again to return they did as they pleased with it—The property forming the subject of the several Indictments upon which I was recently tried was quite distinct from that before alluded to—this was taken from my *Lodgings* just prior to my Escape in 1827 and upon which I was committed for Trial—but as the old adage goes 'Put a Bird in an open Cage and it will make its escape' was verified in me.—

I shall before I conclude state my reason for leaving America for Hobart Town which was solely to gain the Society of an affectionate Wife—I have been blamed by several persons for adopting such a course—here I offered to the Governor my services in the capacity of a Convict for the term of 4 years if he would afterwards allow me to remain there and then be under a sacred pledge, nay, I even offered security to any amount which it was in my power to give that I would not then adopt any means to effect her escape but my offers were of no avail—where could have been the policy of sending the distance of 18,000 miles after an already exiled and almost heartbroken man whose intention it was never again to return to this Country tearing him from his Wife and Family to be arraigned and tried at the Bar of the Old Bailey upon several Capital Indictments pointedly terming him not the Receiver but the actual Thief It therefore seems to have been the determination of a few prejudiced persons to deprive me of my life— I stood my trial upon six of these Indictments at the Bar of the Old Court and providentially before a merciful Jury who returned verdicts of not Guilty upon each successive Indictment—I was then removed to the New Court and tried upon two other Indictments one of which termed him the Receiver and the other again the actual Thief—here my Counsel felt it his duty from the great prejudice which existed in the minds of the Jury to challenge the whole of the 12 first impannelled —unfortunately the next 12 were equally prejudiced—for without a tittle of Evidence establishing the facts I was found Guilty upon both Indictments—Although the summing up of the Evidence by Mr. Serjeant Denman was very impartial and if anything favorable [sic] on my part yet the apparent unanimous disposition of the Jury to find me Guilty was most striking—so much so that it occasioned the following remark from my Counsel Mr. Clarkson—'Guilty! Oh it is Ikey Solomons he must be Guilty—if Gentlemen it had been the case of any other person the result would have been different' there seems to have existed a predetermination in defiance of all Law or Custom to convict me—to convict me as an actual Thief must appear to every unprejudiced mind not only cruel but a thing unprecedented.—

I have omitted to state that just previous to my Trial I applied to the Magistrates through whom my property is still withheld for a few pounds for my subsistence while in prison and to enable me to conduct my defence—but was refused even this indulgence from Magistrates who having the controul [sic] of my property instead of seeing it

M

protected have countenanced the unjustifiable conduct of their Officers in taking away my property and converting a great part thereof to their own use—Although my losses and troubles have been many and unceasing and having suffered much from imprisonment to add to my afflicted mind as well as that of my Wife and Family it is painful to me to observe my injured name day after day unnecessarily inserted in the public papers to add fresh odium to it—I am now of the age of 45 years and from the continual run of troubles which my mind has experienced am reduced to a state of extreme wretchedness —I have had to contend with oppression in every form—my mind is litterally [sic] distracted—let any person look at the foregoing Statement and it must appear that there attaches a fatality to my Family— Victims to injury and oppression.—It is not for myself but for the sake of my unfortunate wife and family that I so much grieve—who never till of late knew the want of a single comfort—but now plunged into poverty and despair—two of the eldest of my poor Children are just setting out in the World and struggling to gain a livelihood by their Trades and the youngest unfit to leave the Breast of its heart broken Mother—is it not enough to shock their young minds and to defeat their hopes and future prospects to see their Father's injured name continually inserted in the public papers under the appelation of 'notorious' as if I were a hardened Murder [sic] or capable of committing the most hardened crimes.

Earnestly entreating your Lordship to pardon the liberty I have thus taken for intruding at such a length upon your justly valuable time,
                    I have the honour to be
                        My Lord,
                            Your Lordships, very obedient humble Servant
                            Isaac Solomons

4 Ward
North Side
Newgate

Endorsement on the petition
Isaac Solomon 45 Old Bailey July Sessions 1830 Receiving Stolen Goods Transported for 14 Years Gaoler's Report—Transported before Nil.

(Public Record Office, H.O. 17/113)

NOTE ON SOURCES AND
FURTHER READING

Evidence for the general picture of crime and criminals presented in this book, and further information, is contained in my *Crime and Industrial Society in the Nineteenth Century*. The Pelican edition has in particular a study of the Whitechapel streets in which Ikey grew up. (The book is called *Urban Crime in Victorian England* in its American paperback edition.)

The best modern study of the police is T. A. Critchley, *A History of Police in England and Wales 900–1966*, but of course this is mainly concerned with the period after the introduction of the Metropolitan Police in 1829—after the end of Isaac Solomons's active career in London. A good account of the pre-Metropolitan police of London is in John Wade's *A Treatise on the Crimes and Police of the Metropolis* published in 1829—I have amplified his description in my introduction to the reprint by Patterson Smith in 1972.

The prisons in this country are described by R. S. E. Hinde, *The British Penal System, 1773–1950*. A. G. L. Shaw, *Convicts and the Colonies*, is a general survey of transportation, and W. D. Forsyth, *Governor Arthur's Convict System, Van Diemen's Land, 1824–36*, and C. Bateson, *The Convict Ships*, provide detailed evidence on narrower topics.

The following sections list the sources of information on the criminals mentioned in this book.

1. ISAAC SOLOMONS

Public Record Office:
Register of Newgate Gaol Pri. Comm. 2/185—Apr., July 1810
  ,, ,, ,, ,, ,, 2/186—Apr., June 1810
  ,, ,, ,, ,, ,, 2/199, p. 153—1827
  ,, ,, ,, ,, ,, 2/201, p. 14—1830
Ordinary's and Surgeon's Notebook Pri. Comm. 2/161—1825–30
Hulks Register H.O. 9/7, p. 12—1810–16
Hulks Accounts T. 38/331, 332, 336, 337—1810–16

Hulks Register H.O. 9/9, p. 55—1831
Out-correspondence, Criminal H.O. 13/25, p. 27—1813
„   „   „   13/28, pp. 252-3—1816
„   „   „   13/29, pp. 85-6—1816
„   „   „   13/49, pp. 8, 25, 26—1827
Out-correspondence, Police H.O. 61/1, pp. 353-5, 360-4, 397-8—
                                                          1828
Criminal Register H.O. 26/36, p. 225—1830
Old Bailey Returns H.O. 16/4, p. 256—1830
Petition from Isaac Solomons H.O. 17/113, Wp16—1831
Transportation Register H.O. 11/8, p. 48—1830
Surgeon's Log, *William Glen Anderson* Ad. 101, Bundle 74(7)—1831
Return of Convicts, Van Diemen's Land H.O. 10/48, p. 179—1832
„   „   „   „   „   „   10/49, p. 171—1833

Archives Office of Tasmania:
Despatches GO 2/5, GO 33/4-7—1828-30
Executive Council Minutes 2/1—1830
Files CSO 1/342/7861, CSO 1/354/8078, CSO 1/430/9642, CSO
    1/820/17494, CSO 5/131/3131—1828-35
Convict Record 31/39, 2/170

Middlesex Records, Greater London Record Office:
Calendar of Indictments 3—June 1810
„   „   5—May 1827
Old Bailey Sessions Roll, June 1810, Indictment 2
„   „   „   „   May 1827, Indictments 283-5
Middlesex Sessions Roll, May 1827, Indictments 486, 349, 350, 457, 315

City of London Record Office:
Sessions Roll, May 1827, Indictments 74-8
Minute Book, July 1830, pp. 16-7

Archives of United Synagogue:
Marriage Register IE-155, p. 106—1807
Births Register IE-112—1820, 1823

Newspapers
Morning Chronicle 14, 21 Sept. 1827

Morning Post 21 Apr. 1810; 15 June 1810; 26 May 1827; 9–14 July 1830; 14 May 1831

The Times 18, 21 Apr. 1810; 26, 28, 29 May 1827; 4, 9 June 1827; 2–14 July 1830; 14 May 1831

Unidentified cutting, *Bow Street 1801–1823*, London Library, p. 26 —Apr. 1810

Colonial Times (Hobart) 20 Nov. 1829; 11 Dec. 1829; 29 Jan. 1830

Launceston Advertiser 16, 23 Nov. 1829; 7 Dec. 1829; 11 Jan. 1830

Tasmanian & Australasian Review 6, 13, 20, 27, Nov. 1829; 4 Dec. 1829; 29 Jan. 1830; 5 Feb. 1830

Other Contemporary Sources

Old Bailey Proceedings 1809–10, pp. 267–8

,,   ,,   ,,   1829–30, pp. 575–7, 592–3, 629–30, 646

,,   ,,   ,,   1830–31, p. 592

Evidence to Select Committee on Police, Parliamentary Papers 1828, VI, pp. 95, 178

Evidence to Select Committee on Secondary Punishment, Parliamentary Papers 1831–2, VII, p. 620

Evidence to Select Committee on Police, Parliamentary Papers 1837, XII, pp. 434–5

Evidence to Select Committee on Transportation, Parliamentary Papers 1837, XIX, p. 159

Annual Register, 1830, pp. 104–7

R. v Isaac Solomons, 1 *Moodie* 292 (*English Reports* 168, 1276)—1830

Playbill for Royal Surrey Theatre, 19 Nov. 1838 (Brit. Mus. Playbills 313)

Fraser's Magazine, vol. vi, pp. 291–2, 490—Nov. 1832

,,   ,,   ,, xxiv, p. 672—Dec. 1841

Adventures, Memoirs, Former Trial, Transportation, and Escapes, of that Notorious Fence, and Receiver of Stolen Goods, Isaac Solomons . . . by a Former Police Officer—1829

The Life and Adventures of Isaac Solomons, the notorious receiver of stolen goods, better known as Ikey Solomons. . .—1830

The Life and Exploits of Ikey Solomons, Swindler, forger, fencer, and brothel-keeper . . . By Moses Hebron . . .—1829

J. Bee, *A Living Picture of London, for 1828, and stranger's guide . . .*, p. 18 —1828

H. Melville, *The History of the Island of Van Diemen's Land . . .*, pp. 266–7—1835

C. Pelham, *The Chronicles of Crime; or, The New Newgate Calendar*
   vol. ii, pp. 235–41—1841

Later References
P. Collins, *Dickens and Crime*, p. 262—1962
M. Gordon, *Jews in Van Diemen's Land*, pp. 40–2—1965
A. G. F. Griffiths, *The Chronicles of Newgate*, vol. ii, pp. 317–21—1884
G. C. Ingleton (ed.), *True Patriots All. . .* , pp. 136–40—1952
M. J. Landa, *The Jew in Drama*, pp. 159–67—1926
L. Lane, 'Dickens' Archetypal Jew' *PMLA*, vol. lxxiii, pp. 94–100—
   1958
H. Levi, *Jewish Characters in Fictional English Literature*, p. 68—1911
C. McNaught, 'Round About Old East London', *East London Observer*,
   17 Apr. 1915, 22 May 1915
M. F. Modder, *The Jew in the Literature of England. . .* , pp. 222–3—1939
A. Morrison, *A Child of the Jago*, ch. 24—1896
E. W. Pugh, *The Charles Dickens Originals*. pp. 241–52—1913
H. Stone, 'Dickens and the Jews', *Victorian Studies*, vol. ii, pp. 223–253
   —1959
Australian Dictionary of Biography, vol. ii, pp. 457–8

2. ANN SOLOMONS

Public Record Office:
Register of Newgate Gaol Pri. Comm. 2/199, p. 254—1827
Old Bailey Returns H.O. 16/4, p. 48—1827
Petitions from Ann Solomons and Joseph Ridley H.O. 17/107, Vm 12
   —1827
Transportation Register H.O. 11/6, p. 312—1828
Surgeon's Log, *Mermaid*, Ad. 101, Bundle 53(3)—1828
Return of Convicts, Van Diemen's Land H.O. 10/48, p. 238—1832
   „   „   „   „   „   „   10/49, p. 234—1833

Archives Office of Tasmania:
Convict Record 40/9

Middlesex Records, Greater London Record Office:
Calendar of Indictments 5—Sept. 1827
Old Bailey Sessions Roll, Sept. 1827, Indictments 306–8

Newspapers
Morning Chronicle 21, 24 Sept, 1827
Morning Post 28 June 1827; 31 Aug 1827; 1–21 Sept. 1827
The Times 4 June 1827; 22, 28 June 1827; 30, 31 Aug. 1827; 12, 21, 24
   Sept. 1827

Old Bailey Proceedings 1826–7, pp. 731–2

3. HENRY SOLOMONS

Public Record Office:
Register of Newgate Gaol Pri. Comm. 2/199, p. 198—1827
Criminal Register H.O. 26/33, p. 200—1827
Old Bailey Returns H.O. 16/4, pp. 38, 46—1827
List of Respites Pri. Comm. 2/190—July 1827

City of London Record Office: Sessions Roll, July 1827
The Times 9, 18 July 1827; 24 Sept. 1827
Old Bailey Proceedings 1826–7, pp. 537–40

4. JOHN SOLOMONS

The Times 2 July 1827

5. BENJAMIN SOLOMONS

The Times 25, 29 Oct. 1827

6. OTHER CRIMINALS MENTIONED

Joel Joseph—see 1810 references for Isaac Solomons, and *Public Record
   Office:* Transportation Register H.O. 11/2, p. 19—1811
Richard Hook, Michael Gerain and William Hall—
   Public Record Office: Hulks Register H.O. 9/7, pp. 8, 9, 12—1809-16
                Hulks Accounts T. 38/331, 336,337—1810–16
                Out-correspondence, Criminal H.O. 13/28,
                pp. 252–3—1816
Jonas Solomon—
   Public Record Office: Hulks Register H.O. 9/7, p. 19—1812–16
                Out-correspondence, Criminal H.O. 13/29,
                pp. 85–6—1816

Dick the Adelphi Boy—
 H. Mayhew, *London Labour and the London Poor*, vol. iv, pp. 318–20—
Frank Cass & Co. Ltd. 1967.

Nelson—
 H. Brandon ed., *Poverty, Mendicity and Crime. . .*, pp. 112, 114, 137
  —1839

Another Isaac Solomons—
 Old Bailey Proceedings 1826–7, pp. 562–3

John Puddifoot—
 Public Record Office: Circuit Letters H.O. 6/15—1830

Convicts mentioned by Rev. R. H. S. Cotton—
 Public Record Office: Ordinary's and Surgeon's Notebook Pri. Comm.
  2/161—1825–30

CHRONOLOGY

About 1785		Probable date of birth of Isaac Solomons.
1786–8		Possible date of birth of Hannah (Ann) Julian, later Mrs. Isaac Solomons.
1807	7th July	Marriage of Isaac and Ann at the Great Synagogue, Duke's Place.
1808		Probable date of birth of John Solomons.
1809–10		Probable date of birth of Moses Solomons.
1810	17th Apr.	Isaac is arrested, in company with Joel Joseph.
	19th	Isaac & Joel appear at Bow Street Police Office, and are committed to Newgate Prison.
	June	Isaac & Joel are tried and convicted at the Old Bailey.
	14th	They are sentenced to transportation for life.
	10th Jul.	They enter the *Zealand* hulk off Sheerness.
1811	10th Mar.	Joel Joseph leaves the *Zealand* for *Admiral Gambier*.
	12th May	*Admiral Gambier* sails for New South Wales.
1814	Jan.	All convicts in *Zealand* transferred to *Retribution*.
1816	28th June	Isaac Solomons released from *Retribution* in error
	15th Jul.	He re-enters *Retribution*.
	26th Oct.	He is given a free pardon.
	31st Oct.	He is released from *Retribution*.
1818		Probable date of birth of David Solomons.
1820	12th Jan.	Birth of Nancy (Anne) Solomons, later Mrs. J. G. W. Wilson.
1823	4th Oct.	Birth of Sarah Solomons, later Mrs. G. B. Levy.
1825	22/23 Dec.	Burglary at McCabe & Strachan's warehouse.
1826	May	Charles Strachan calls with searchwarrant at Ikey's house in Bell Lane, Spitalfields—Ikey escapes.
1826		Probable date of birth of Mark Solomons.
1827	March	Isaac Solomons lodges with Jane Oades in Islington.
	23rd Apr.	He is recognised and arrested by James Lea, an officer of Lambeth-Street Court, and lodged in Whitechapel watch-house.
	25th	Ikey's first appearance at Lambeth Street Police Office.

1827 15th May — Hearings at Lambeth Street completed—Ikey is committed to Newgate for trial at the Old Bailey.

25th — Ikey escapes from custody; the house of his father Henry is searched and stolen goods found.

28th — James Isaacs, Ikey's agent, appears at Lambeth Street to exculpate himself of involvement in the arrest.

3rd Jun. — Ann Solomons applies to Lambeth Street magistrates for help in recovering money from James Isaacs.

19th — Ann is arrested for receiving stolen goods.

20th — Ann appears at Lambeth Street and is committed to New Prison, Clerkenwell, for further enquiries.

27th — Ann re-appears at Lambeth Street and is discharged.

29th — John Solomons, Isaac's eldest son, is arrested on a charge of receiving stolen goods.

30th — He appears at Lambeth Street and is discharged.

6th Jul. — Henry Solomons, Isaac's father, is arrested for receiving stolen goods.

7th — Henry appears before the Lord Mayor at the Mansion House and is committed to Newgate for trial at the Old Bailey.

14th — Henry is tried at the Old Bailey and convicted; sentence is respited to the next sessions.

29th Aug. — Ann Solomons's house in Bell Lane is searched and counterfeit money and stolen goods found; she is arrested, together with Moses, her second son, and Clara Brown, her servant.

4th Sept. — The three accused appear at Hatton Garden Police Office.

12th — They appear again; Moses and Clara are discharged, but Ann is committed to Newgate for trial at the Old Bailey.

18th — Ann Solomons appears at the Old Bailey, but the case is put back.

20th — Ann is convicted on one charge of receiving stolen goods and acquitted on two others.

23rd — Ann and Henry Solomons appear for sentence at the end of the sessions; she is sentenced to 14 years' transportation, he to 6 months' imprisonment in the House of Correction.

1827	24 Oct.	Benjamin Solomons, Isaac's brother, appears before the Lord Mayor at the Mansion House charged with receiving stolen goods; he is remanded in custody and sent to the Compter.
	28th	He re-appears before the Lord Mayor and is discharged.
1828	8th Jan.	Ann's petition to the King is marked 'Nil'.
	21st	Ann is examined by surgeon of convict ship to determine if she is fit to stand the journey to Australia.
	24th Feb.	*Mermaid*, with Ann and her younger children on board, sails from London.
	spring	Isaac Solomons (our Ikey or another) is engaged in negotiation with Bishop the police officer over the return of stolen property.
	1st Apr.	*Mermaid* crosses the Equator.
	11th May	Mark Solomons in *Mermaid's* sick-bay for 7 days— 'diarrhoea'.
	12th	Anne Solomons in *Mermaid's* sick-bay for 14 days— 'febris'.
	27th June	*Mermaid* reaches Hobart, Van Diemen's Land.
	5th Jul.	Ann and her children disembark from *Mermaid*.
	16th	Isaac Solomons, under the name 'Slowman', sails from Rio de Janeiro in *Coronet*.
	6th Oct.	Ikey arrives in Van Diemen's Land and lodges with the Newmans.
	17th	Ikey's arrival reported to the Colonial Office by the Lieutenant-Governor.
	Nov.	Solomonses and Newmans quarrel; Ann is returned to the Factory.
	19th Dec.	Lieutenant-Governor rejects idea of assigning Ann to Isaac or John Solomons.
1829	12th Mar.	Isaac, John and others enter into bond that Ann will not leave the Colony.
	16th	Lieutenant-Governor allows Ann to be assigned to her husband.
	23rd Apr.	Colonial Office notifies Home Office that Isaac is in Van Diemen's Land.
	6th May	Home Office sends warrants for Ikey's arrest to Colonial Office.

1829	7th May	Colonial Office sends warrants to Lieutenant-Governor.
	1st Nov.	Warrants arrive in Van Diemen's Land.
	by 8th	Ikey is arrested, but applies for a writ of *habeas corpus*.
	9th	*Habeas corpus* proceedings begin in Supreme Court of Van Diemen's Land.
	20th	Executive Council decides on action to be taken if *habeas corpus* is granted.
1830	2nd Jan.	*Habeas corpus* proceedings end: Chief Justice grants writ, subject to heavy bail which Ikey cannot find.
	by 23rd	Lieutenant-Governor issues his own warrant for Ikey's arrest and orders his return to the United Kingdom.
	25th	*Prince Regent* sails from Hobart, with Isaac Solomons on board as a prisoner.
	27th Jun.	Isaac re-enters Newgate Prison.
	8th Jul.	First indictments against Ikey are tried at the Old Bailey.
	12th	Ikey is convicted on the McCabe & Strachan charge; point of law reserved for the judges.
	13th	Last day of Ikey's trials at Old Bailey—he is convicted on a further charge but sentence is respited.
1831		Ikey Solomons's case considered by the judges and decided against him.
	12th May	Ikey appears again at the Old Bailey and is sentenced to 14 years' transportation.
	31st	Ikey is sent from Newgate to Gosport, where he spends the night in *York* hulk.
	1st June	Ikey enters *William Glen Anderson*.
	2nd	*William Glen Anderson* leaves Portsmouth for Van Diemen's Land.
	1st Nov.	*William Glen Anderson* arrives at Hobart.
	Nov.	Isaac Solomons becomes a javelin man at Richmond Gaol.
1832		Ann Solomons is assigned to one of her sons.
	19th Nov.	Isaac is punished for 'abusive language . . . and disorderly conduct'.
	5th Dec.	Isaac is punished for 'preferring false and malicious charges'.

1834	18th Jul.	Isaac is sent to work in the office at Port Arthur Penal Settlement.
1834–5		Ann Solomons becomes the mistress of George Madden.
1835	June	Ikey is granted a ticket of leave and moves to New Norfolk.
	3rd Jul.	Ikey is admonished for 'drunkenness and violent conduct towards his family'.
	16th	Quarrel in the Solomons family—David assaults his father.
	20th	Ann is committed to the Factory for 'using opprobrious epithets to her Husband and otherwise ill-treating him'.
	8th Sept.	Ann is released from the Factory.
	5th Nov.	Ann is granted a ticket of leave.
1836	18th Feb.	Isaac is reprimanded for 'obscene language'.
1838		Isaac is allowed to live in Hobart Town.
1840	4th May	Anne Solomons marries John G. W. Wilson.
	27th	Isaac and Ann are granted conditional pardons.
1844		Isaac receives a certificate of freedom.
1847	27th Jan.	Sarah Solomons marries Godfrey B. Levy.
1850	3rd Sept.	Burial of Isaac Solomons in Hobart Town.

INDEX